# Lucile Mathevon, RSCJ
(1793-1876) FRIEND OF THE POTAWATOMI

Carolyn Osiek, RSCJ
and
Helen Rosenthal, RSCJ

Society of the Sacred Heart
St. Louis, Missouri

Lucile Mathevon, RSCJ (1793-1876)
Friend of the Potawatomi
© 2022 Carolyn Osiek, RSCJ and Helen Rosenthal, RSCJ
All rights reserved.

No part of this book may be used or reproduced by any means, graphic, electronic, or mechanical, including photocopying, recording, taping or by any information storage retrieval system without the written permission of the authors, except in the case of brief quotations embodied in critical articles and reviews.

ISBN: 978-1-7364924-1-3
Book Design: Peggy Nehmen
Photos: Society of the Sacred Heart Archives

Printed in the United States of America.

Published by:

4120 Forest Park Ave.
St. Louis, Missouri 63108
rscj.org

## CONTENTS

Introduction ........................................................................... 1
Beginnings in France ............................................................ 3
First Years in America ........................................................ 15
Superior at St. Charles ....................................................... 23
Journey to the Potawatomi ............................................... 40
Life at Sugar Creek ............................................................. 47
Move to St. Mary's ............................................................. 56
Living the Mission at St. Mary's ...................................... 59
First Return to St. Louis .................................................... 62
Official Vicariate Visits ..................................................... 65
Years in Exile from St. Mary's ......................................... 78
Return and Final Years ..................................................... 84
Conclusion .......................................................................... 93
Epilogue ............................................................................... 95
Appendices .......................................................................... 96
   1. Journal of the Crossing, 1821-1822
      by Lucile Mathevon, RSCJ ...................................... 96
   2. First Account of the Foundation at
      Sugar Creek, by Lucile Mathevon ......................... 109
   3. Second Account of the Foundation at
      Sugar Creek, by Lucile Mathevon ......................... 115
   4. Memories of Marie Monzert, RSCJ
      (after 1869) ................................................................ 131

5. Memories of Elizabeth Schrader, RSCJ
   (after 1879) .................................................................. 136
6. Memories of Ellen Craney, RSCJ
   (after 1879) .................................................................. 145

Primary Sources .................................................................. 149

Index of Biographical Notes ................................................ 153

# INTRODUCTION

In a letter of September 28, 1935, Louise Callan, RSCJ, then nearing completion of her own doctoral dissertation that would become *The Society of the Sacred Heart in North America* in 1937, replied to a letter of Catherine McShane, RSCJ, who had asked her for ideas for another dissertation topic in the history of the Society of the Sacred Heart in North America.[1] Mother Callan recommended "The RSCJ among the Potowatomi [sic] Indians." She wrote:

> And through the whole of this, like a golden thread binding it into unity, runs the character of our greatest Indian missionary nun, Mother Lucile Mathevon – a novice of Mother Duchesne, foundress of the house of St. Charles (1828), and for about 35 years the very heart and soul of the Indian Mission. She is just glorious – a Dauphinoise, but so different from Mother Duchesne – yet a SAINT. You see where my heart lies. I should thrill to write it all myself....You can imagine how little of all this I could include in one chapter of my dissertation, not 50 typed pages.

---

1 Instead, Mother McShane chose a topic in colonial Jesuit history: *Hernando de Santarén: Founder of the Jesuit Missions of the Sierra Madre*, Ph.D. Thesis, University of California, 1939.

Lucile Mathevon has not gone completely unnoticed, however. There were testimonies about her heroism and holiness from others who had lived with her.[2] In 1926, Celeste Thompson, RSCJ, had written a 172-page biographical portrait as her master's thesis, "Mother Lucile Mathevon among the Potawatomi" (M.S. Loyola University, Chicago). Sometime after 1970, otherwise unknown Mary O'Dowd wrote a shorter unpublished sketch, "Lucile Mathevon: Years among the Potawatomi." Yet there is a great deal of irony in the attention paid to St. Philippine finally arriving at her dream at Sugar Creek, though her residence there lasted just less than one year, while Lucile Mathevon lived out that dream for more than thirty years. Lucile's life was long, full, and heroic. It is worth retelling, this time begun by Helen Rosenthal, RSCJ, and completed by Carolyn Osiek, RSCJ.

---

[2] Ellen Craney, RSCJ (1853-1931); Marie Rose Monzert, RSCJ (1828-1903); Elizabeth (Elisabeth) Schrader (Shrader, Schroeder), RSCJ (1829-1903). See bibliography.

# BEGINNINGS IN FRANCE: GOD'S CALL (1793-1821)

Lucile Mathevon was born near the city of Lyon, France, on January 6, 1793, daughter of devout Catholics, Jean-Marie Mathevon and Catherine Savoie, who risked their lives to give sanctuary to priests during the Reign of Terror. Little is known of Lucile's childhood except for a memory that she retold years later. She remembered at about five years of age, being present for a meeting of bishops and priests in their family home. She had entered quietly, and when the bishops saw her, they caressed and blessed her. The account in the *Annual Letters* implies that this memory occurred during the Reign of Terror, and therefore when the bishops and priests were in hiding. However, the Reign of Terror lasted from September 5, 1793 to July 28, 1794, ending when Lucile was less than two years old, so the memory must have come from following years.[3]

Her education was entrusted to a pious lady in Lyon, under the direction of Abbé de la Marche, who was by that time renowned as the secret spiritual guide of the Carmelite martyrs of Compiègne in 1794. He also had connections, if he was not a member, with the Fathers of the Faith, the group of priests, including Joseph Varin and Louis Barat, who followed Jesuit spirituality and in fact became Jesuits as soon as the Company was restored in France in 1814, though Father de la Marche

---

3   It is related correctly in *Quelques contemporaines*, 118.

apparently did not join them.[4] In the years just before that, de la Marche was in Lyon, known for conducting pilgrimages to the great shrine of Our Lady on the hilltop at Fourvière, an important place of pilgrimage since the Middle Ages. The destination then was not the magnificent church that dominates the hill today, built from 1872 to 1896, but the earlier, smaller one of the late sixteenth century, which still stands modestly beside its much more imposing younger sister. Lucile said that every time she went there, she received a special grace from Mary. Father de la Marche put Lucile at the end of the procession when there were few because she had such a good strong singing voice that people would hear her and come out to join the pilgrimage. She related that on one occasion, there were only a few people ready to climb the hill with him to the church. They went, collecting people along the way. By the time they arrived and then descended again, there were 5,000, to whom he then preached a retreat.

Lucile spent much time working with the poor and needy, going several times a week with her servant to visit prisons and hospitals. When she lacked resources, she would get them from friends. While she was searching for a direction in life, a priest, likely one of the Fathers of the Faith, told her about the Society of the Sacred Heart, not yet present in Lyon. She presented herself at Sainte-Marie d'en Haut in Grenoble, where the house journal, then kept by Philippine Duchesne, records the entry of Mlle. Mathevon on July 14, 1813. The *Annual Letters* say that she was "received by Mother Duchesne," something of a misinterpretation. Philippine was present in the community as assistant superior, but Genevieve Deshayes was superior at that time. The

---

4  Cahier 1.215-216. He also had connections with Madeleine Sophie Barat and the Society of the Sacred Heart, calling himself its oldest friend (Kilroy, pp. 115, 467-68).

Older Basilica of Notre Dame de Fourvière. Fourviere.org

mistress of novices from December 1812 was Josephine Bigeu, replaced in that position by Therese Maillucheau a year after Lucile's entrance, in July 1814. While Philippine was assistant superior, it was not she who was in the position to receive a new postulant.

Though Lucile was certainly aware of Mother Duchesne in the community, she therefore spent the time in the noviceship under the direction of Mothers Bigeu and Maillucheau and made her first vows on April 2, 1815. Philippine would have been present. She must have shared with Lucile during those years her ardent desire for the American mission. That dream was not yet envisioned as possible when six months later, on October 25, 1815, Mothers Deshayes and Duchesne left Grenoble to attend the second general council of the Society in Paris. There, Philippine was elected secretary general and remained in Paris. As far as we know, she never returned to Grenoble before leaving for America on February 8, 1818. No letters between her and Lucile are extant, but by 1820, it is clear from Mother Barat's correspondence that Lucile is marked for the American mission.

The following month after the departure of Mothers Deshayes and Duchesne for Paris in October 1815, another postulant entered at Sainte-Marie whose destiny would cross that of Philippine Duchesne and Lucile Mathevon. On November 25, 1815, Eugenie Audé entered the Society in Grenoble. Destined to be one of Philippine's companions in 1818, she too would be an important part of the matrix of the American foundations, foundress in Grand Coteau and St. Michael, Louisiana, and later, assistant general.

By November 1816, Lucile, still in Grenoble, was involved in family business, needing to dispose of property in anticipation of making final vows. The house journal of Sainte-Marie records on November 15 that Mother Lucile Mathevon has made her testament, one part to Mother Moulin[5] and the other to her family.[6]

---

5 Marie Moulin (Moulins), RSCJ, was born about 1785 and entered the Society in Grenoble, September 1, 1809. She made first vows February 2, 1816, and profession November 1, 1820. She went to Lille in 1830, where she died February 1, 1831. This is the information in the *Circulaire* at the time of her death, GASSH. There is no explanation for the long period between entrance and first vows.
6 The French text says to her *parents*, which can mean the same as English parents or more generally, family. By 1820, her mother and father were no longer living (Madeleine Sophie Barat to Philippine, April 12, 1820).

It was not unusual at the time for religious to make their wills in favor of another religious, absent legal recognition of newly established religious orders. It is not known why Lucile chose Marie Moulin. Their time in Grenoble overlapped for about seven years. By December 1820, Lucile was still dealing with complicated business with regard to inherited property and negotiations with family. In a letter then, Mother Barat urged her to simplify matters in favor of the family. Later, in September 1821, on the eve of Lucile's departure for America, Mother Barat questioned why she had chosen someone older than she, who would probably die first, and their distance from each other would create a great inconvenience. Mother Barat encouraged her to sell the property or redo the will in favor of someone younger or even better, in favor of an agent of the Society, as Philippine had done. We do not have Lucile's response.

On November 21, 1816, Therese Maillucheau became superior at Sainte-Marie, and Lucile continued in the community. She would have heard about the departure from Paris on February 8, 1818, of Philippine Duchesne, Eugenie Audé, Octavie Berthold, Catherine Lamarre, and Marguerite Manteau, first to Bordeaux and then on March 19, to America. On May 29, the very day that the first missionary band, Philippine and her four companions, landed in New Orleans, back in Grenoble, Lucile made her final profession of vows. They would not have learned of the coincidence until much later, but by this time, Lucile was certainly indicating her desire to be a missionary in their footsteps. Mother Barat wrote to Philippine on August 21, 1818, that "Sr. Lucile is burning to join you: she is a person of solid virtue, she holds the day school very well, but how can she learn English?"[7]

---

[7] De Charry, letter 99 (Eng. 2.1, p. 76).

With or without English, by April 12, 1820, Lucile's departure, along with that of Anna Xavier Murphy,[8] was announced in a letter of Madeleine Sophie to Philippine. With regard to the Irishwoman Anna Murphy, she was still a novice in Paris at the time, and "we are teaching her French as far as we can. She is thirty-plus years old and comes from Ireland. The Irish character resembles ours to a remarkable degree." (She was in fact twenty-seven.) Of Lucile, Mother Barat wrote: "She has neither mother nor father, is genuinely virtuous and ready to do anything."

Philippine was not impressed with the choice, however. There must have been previous discussion that also included the possibility of Hélène Dutour. Four months earlier, Philippine had written to Mother Barat on December 16, 1819: "Mothers Lucile and Dutour are not appropriate for coming here: it needs more external style and talents, and especially knowledge of English." Philippine's diffidence about her own social skills is reflected here. Mother Barat had probably not yet received this letter; in any event, she ignored it. Lucile was practically on her way. Hélène Dutour would also come eventually, but not until 1827, and when she did, her participation in the American mission was problematic.[9] Meanwhile, preparations continued. On July 10, 1820, Mother Barat told Lucile that she must learn

---

8  Anna Murphy, born in 1793 in Cork, Ireland, entered the Society in May 1820 in Paris and made her first vows on November 6, 1821, in view of going to America. Arrived in New Orleans, she went directly to Grand Coteau, where she made her final profession on May 14, 1822, the first final profession of a Religious of the Sacred Heart in the New World. She was superior there from 1825 until her death in 1836.

9  Hélène Dutour, RSCJ, born 1787 in Savoy, entered in Grenoble 1813 and made her profession there in 1818 with Lucile Mathevon. Once in America, she was quickly superior at the new foundation of Lafourche, Louisiana, where her determination to make the school of top quality caused conflict with nearby St. Michael, and she ran up impossible debt. She left there for Grand Coteau in 1831 and died in Natchitoches in 1847. The school at Lafourche closed the following year, 1832.

English, that Philippine insists on it: "a language so difficult that even she can't learn it." There is still a question of selling property and what to do with the proceeds. The new foundation at Lyon could certainly use it, adds Mother Barat, or she could give it to her nieces and nephews.

A year later, preparations are still ongoing. On July 17, 1821, Mother Barat wrote to tell Lucile to put all her business affairs in order and gather some money.

> Ah! how your mothers need the help that you will bring. They are waiting for you impatiently. Alas! They think you are already in route and you are still far from being ready. I say far because of the need they have of you....the time is drawing near, toward the month of November, I hope. Meanwhile, do not lose a moment to get closer to God and make yourself ready for his plans of goodness and mercy.

Sometime before November 8, 1821, Lucile left Sainte-Marie in Grenoble, the home she had known since 1813, for Paris. She must have already known Mother Barat, who had been to Grenoble more than once during the years Lucile was there, but in Paris she met for the first time the Irishwoman, Anna Xavier Murphy, who would be her companion on the voyage of several months. They left Paris on the eighth of the month for Bordeaux to await embarkation. They were to wait there for a full month. On November 17, Mother Barat wrote to her in Bordeaux, giving news of various packages on the way and how to handle various relationships there. She was happy that Lucile and Anna were safely with Mother Lalanne.[10] There were others

---

10  Catherine Suzanne Felicity Dudevant Lalanne (1756-1835) founded an orphanage

in Bordeaux for them to meet, and Lucile's final letter of thanks before embarkation acknowledges them: Louis Barat, Mother Barat's brother, and Victoire Fournier and Mrs. Dubourg, sister and sister-in-law of Bishop Louis William Dubourg, with whom they would be serving in America.

Three weeks later, on November 29, Mother Barat's next letter enclosed the list of contents for her baggage that needed to be attached to avoid customs. Most of the letter, however, was about the story of Rosalie Meneyroux, also known as Josephine, a young woman who had tried her vocation, faltered, and with encouragement from Louis Barat but no permission from Sophie, had sailed for the American mission. Mother Barat figured the two would encounter her in New Orleans, but in fact, she had left the day before for Grand Coteau. Mother Barat's advice was to be good to her. She believed that Josephine had a vocation, but was just lacking in judgment on certain points. "Truly," she wrote, "her attachment to the Society touches me, and I feel sorry for her."[11]

Finally, on December 6, 1821, at four o'clock in the afternoon, they embarked at the port of Pauillac, the same place from which Philippine Duchesne and her four companions had embarked three years earlier. From the ship just before they sailed, Lucile wrote a quick letter to Mother Bigeu, her former novice director in Grenoble, entrusted to Mother Lalanne in

---

in Bordeaux, and on the death of her husband in 1816, brought the school to the Society of the Sacred Heart in 1818, later in the year than the embarkation of the first missionaries to America in late March. She made her vows in the Society in 1819 and remained in Bordeaux. She was able to give hospitality to Lucile and Anna Murphy while they waited to embark.

11 Josephine arrived in New Orleans on Christmas Eve and stayed with the Ursulines until February 1, only the day before the arrival of Lucile and Anna, when she went unannounced to Grand Coteau. There is no indication that she deliberately left before them. She was appreciated at Grand Coteau, but returned to France in May and disappeared from the records.

Bordeaux, with the report that among the passengers were three women with children ages eleven, five, and two, and another woman who was not well. There were probably eighteen passengers total on board, including a Mr. Nagliss, not listed, owner of all the freight on board and probably of the ship itself. He was an Irishman from Cork now resident in Philadelphia and knew the Murphy family, so that there were great exchanges between him and Anna. In Pauillac, they had dined with the church pastor, who had an Irish assistant, to Anna's delight.

Both Lucile and Anna kept an account of the Atlantic crossing. When the ship sailed on December 7, Lucile wrote to Mother Bigeu: "I felt a great sorrow leaving France. I would not have believed it, never having had that thought, but our good Master wished to use it for his glory; I made a generous sacrifice at once. The day was very beautiful." The next day, she was the first to be sick and have to leave the table.

Lucile's account is rather a straightforward reporting of the facts, while Anna comments more extensively.[12] There were lively conversations among the passengers, most of them Protestant, and Anna Xavier, the fluent English speaker, seems to have carried on a virtual ministry of spiritual direction. In her account, she tells of Lucile's fright during storms, while she, of course, was thrilled by them. Anna makes fun of Lucile's fear, recounting that Lucile sometimes jumped from her bed and stretched out her arms crying for mercy. Once the waves came so high that the lower area inside, including their beds, was completely swamped. In her account, Lucile admits her fear and

---

12 See Appendix I. Lucile's account of the journey: French copy GASSH A.II.2.j, Box 3: *Lettres intéressantes,* cahier 1, pp. 272-280. Paisant L., 117, pp. 438-446. For the complete text of Anna Xavier Murphy's account, see Mary Blish, RSCJ, and Carolyn Osiek, RSCJ, *Anna Xavier Murphy, RSCJ (1793-1836): Missionary to Louisiana.* St. Louis: Society of the Sacred Heart, 2021, pp. 84-94.

her admiration of Anna, who could sleep through the worst of a storm, while Lucile spent the nights in prayer.

On December 12:

> The sea struck the sides at every moment; a wave came up to the window of the cabin where I was sitting. I was covered with water; at that moment, I thought I was drowning. Never will I forget the day of the 12$^{th}$, and the night; every time I saw the captain I asked for news of the weather: "Bad, madam, bad; but do not fear, there is no danger." Finally, during the night, I thought I heard the word "danger"—"What is that?" He laughed at my fear and said to me: "No danger; sleep, madam, sleep."

After having passed Cuba, they were followed for four hours on January 5 by pirates, whom they were finally able to escape, a favor they attributed to the intercession of the Virgin Mary and recently deceased Aloysia Jouve.[13]

On January 30, they were becalmed at the mouth of the Mississippi. A passing steamboat from New York took all the passengers on board on February 1. Their baggage remained behind on the ship and took some time to arrive eventually. The two religious were again courteously treated on the steamboat, and Lucile in her report back to France told of her amazement at the quiet manners of the men and that, though the two nuns were with the fifty passengers for twenty-four hours, they did not hear a single swear word. The steamboat arrived in New Orleans at ten o'clock in the morning on February 2.

---

13 Euphrosine Jouve, RSCJ, Philippine's niece, who took the name Aloysia upon her entrance at Sainte-Marie, died a heroic and holy death at the age of twenty-five on January 21, 1821. Lucile was probably there at the time of her death.

Their mentor Mr. Nagliss took the two religious to the Ursulines, who received them with the same gracious hospitality with which they had welcomed the five missionaries who had come to them three years before, and Josephine Meneyroux in the previous months. Bishop Dubourg was in the city, and came to see them just an hour after their arrival to welcome them and tell them that they would now be separated, Anna to Grand Coteau and Lucile to Saint Louis, after they had recovered from their voyage in New Orleans. Lucile compared it to the separation of Paul and Barnabas after traveling together (Acts 15:39).

The next day they were up early and joined the Ursuline sisters for morning Office. Both described their weeks in New Orleans in their continuing journals. The Ursuline community consisted of sixteen sisters, about half of whom were elderly and infirm. Lucile and Anna were present for the election of a new superior on February 10 and the death of the former superior a month later. They participated in the life of the community and the school that the Ursulines operated.

The two missionaries parted company on March 12, never to see each other again. By this time, Lucile had received a letter from Mother Duchesne welcoming her to St. Louis. While Anna Xavier set off for Grand Coteau in the company of two postulants (one of them Carmelite Landry),[14] Lucile left New Orleans when the Mississippi had thawed sufficiently, on a steamboat (not "Flat-Boat" as indicated in the *AL*), traveling in the company of John Mullanphy, the rich Saint Louis merchant

---

14 Carmelite Landry, RSCJ (1792-1852) was born in Lafourche, Louisiana. She had entered as a postulant with the Ursulines, but was so attracted to Anna Xavier that she asked to enter the Society instead, the first native-born woman from Louisiana to do so. She entered as a coadjutrix sister, but Philippine Duchesne, who gave her the habit the following August while visiting, was so impressed with her that she changed her status to choir religious. She made her profession in Grand Coteau in 1825 and remained there for the rest of her life.

who would later be a benefactor to the Saint Louis houses. Soon into the trip, the boat had a misadventure and broke its paddle-wheel, delaying the trip by twelve days, which they spent in New Madrid. There Lucile saw Indians[15] for the first time. They came to see her, making many signs, and seemed pleased by her black robe, though she could not communicate with them. The travelers finally arrived in Saint Louis on April 14, 1822. Lucile was met by Father Anduze and General Pratte,[16] who had been host for the five who arrived in 1818. The next day, General Pratte and his son and daughter took Lucile to Florissant. They arrived at two o'clock in the afternoon.

Part of one of Lucile's letters to Mother Barat on June 20, 1822, indicates that it may also have been planned that she go to Louisiana, not Missouri. It is possible that Eugenie Audé was exerting pressure to have her there. But Bishop Dubourg from the moment he met her said that she was to go to St. Louis, and Philippine also directed her by letter to come to Florissant.

---

15 While today Native Americans is the preferred name for indigenous peoples, Europeans of Lucile's time used Indians, or in French often *sauvages*, a term that did not carry negative connotations, but rather romantic connotations of the "noble savage." Here, the designation Indians is retained, as being closer to the language of the day.

16 Aristide Anduze, C.M., came from France in 1818, was ordained in St. Louis in 1821, and spent time in Missouri and Louisiana before returning to France in 1844. Bernard Pratte (1771-1836) had served in the War of 1812 and made a fortune in trade. He had seven children, one of whom was fourth mayor of St. Louis in 1844-1846. Two of his daughters, Emilie and Therese, were the first boarders in the school in St. Charles.

# FIRST YEARS IN AMERICA: FLORISSANT (1822-1827)

The little community in Florissant received Lucile with overwhelming joy. They had received word only on March 25 of the arrival in New Orleans of the two from France. There were probably eleven in the Florissant community at the time. Four of the original five were still there: Philippine Duchesne, Octavie Berthold, Catherine Lamarre, and Marguerite Manteau. The fifth member, Eugenie Audé, had left for the foundation at Grand Coteau in August of the previous year with novice Mary Layton. There were also six novices. Emilie (Josephine) Saint-Cyr would make her vows three months later and go to Louisiana later in the year. Eulalie (Regis) Hamilton would make one of the most solid contributors to the building up of the American mission.[17] Mary Frances Mullanphy, a distant relative of John Mullanphy, would go to Grand Coteau in 1822; she did not stay in the Society. Three others were unfortunately destined for early deaths in Louisiana: Mary Ann Summers (1826), Eulalie (Regis)'s sister, Mathilde (Xavier) Hamilton (1827), and Judith (Ignace)

---

17 Eulalie Hamilton, born 1805 in Ste. Genevieve, Missouri, was a boarding student in Florissant along with her sister, Mathilde (Xavier). She entered the Society at Florissant in 1821, one of Philippine's first and most loved novices, taking the name Regis. She was professed in 1826 and served at the City House as mistress general, assistant, and superior, then as superior in St. Charles when Philippine arrived in 1842. In 1847, she went to Canada, then Philadelphia and Detroit, to Philippine's dismay, but returned to St. Charles in 1851 at Philippine's request and was there for her death in 1852. Regis died in Chicago in 1888.

Labruyère (1831). One of the novices at St. Ferdinand, upon their arrival, wrote in an account to Paris that the house was very poor, but that they were so overjoyed to welcome a mother from France that "we would have been so happy to sleep under the beds to give them what we had. The more we suffered privations, the greater was the joy. A holy gaiety animated our recreations. There was never a word of complaint in these meetings, where the most cordial abandonment reigned." [*AL* 1877, p. 272]

Octavie Berthold reported to Mother Barat on June 29, 1822, that Lucile

> is also tested not only by the extreme heat but by the privation of a thousand little conveniences or adornments that serve only to bring out her virtue and the goodness of her heart, which is shown everywhere. She is excellent, extremely docile, hiding her mortification so it is even more meritorious. Indeed, she is the one necessary for our Mother (Philippine) to replace Sister Eugenie, whose absence is felt intensely, to keep the house going.
>
> We really hope that our dear sister's trunk comes soon. The trousseau she was given for the voyage was made of impractical items, and she even slept without sheets on the ship because the young sister in charge of the vestry in Grenoble forgot them.[18]

Not a word of any of this in Lucile's own letters. In her letter of July 20, 1822, to Mother Barat, Lucile reported that the heat was difficult, but so far it was her only cross. She was teaching

---
18 Paisant, L. 129, pp. 478-479.

forty-three day students, good students, most of whom wanted to enter the Society. Mother Duchesne had accepted one, and this spurred on the others. The sacramental life of the parish was going well. The pastor of the church next door was Father Delacroix,[19] who had already been on mission to the Osage. Lucile noted that to Mother Barat. It was the first time Lucile learned of the direct possibility of a specific Indian mission.

For the next six years, Lucile was a member of the community at St. Ferdinand, with Philippine Duchesne as superior, until Philippine's departure in May 1827 for the new foundation in St. Louis. She took with her Irish-born Mary Ann O'Connor, who had made first vows in 1825, and an orphan, Mary Knapp, who was under their care, and would be first in the new orphanage there.[20]

Sophie Barat wrote to Lucile a few months after her arrival in Florissant, on July 20, 1822, expressing her hope that Lucile would be Philippine's support and consolation through her zeal and devotion to the work of the Heart of Jesus there. Perhaps it was Lucile's presence now at St. Ferdinand that enabled Philippine to feel that she could undertake a long journey. On

---

19 Charles Delacroix (1792-1869), born in Belgium and ordained in France, arrived in 1818 and was pastor of St. Ferdinand in 1819, when the religious moved there from St. Charles. He vacated his house for them until theirs was built, and lived in the corn crib of the bishop's farm. He was instrumental in the foundation of St. Michael, Louisiana, where he was pastor in 1824. He returned to Europe in 1839. Seventeen of Philippine Duchesne's letters to him are extant, and an indication of how much she revered him is that the last six were written to him after he had returned to Europe, one from the Potawatomi mission and the rest during her years at St. Charles.

20 Benefactor John Mullanphy had offered the land and some subsidy for the new foundation, on the condition that it would house up to twenty orphan girls, for whom he would provide $10 upon entrance and $5 yearly for each. Girls could be accepted between ages four and eight and could remain until age eighteen. It is clear from the letters of application, preserved in USCA, that "orphan" did not necessarily mean children without parents, but often meant with impoverished parents unable to support them. Mary Knapp later entered the Society, was professed in Grand Coteau in 1853, and died at St. Michael in 1881.

the same day, Philippine departed for Louisiana for her first visit to the new foundation at Grand Coteau, founded less than a year earlier, taking with her Sisters Emilie Saint-Cyr and Mary Mullanphy to stay there, and a boarding student, Therese Pratte, for a visit to her beloved Mother Eugenie, foundress at Grand Coteau the previous year. Octavie Berthold, assistant superior, remained in charge in Florissant.

Like almost everyone else in those years, Lucile quickly succumbed to fever, trembling, she reported, for three, four and six hours every day during a whole month. On September 5, she had been one of several sick with fever but was now better, but again on October 6, she was down with fever, along with Octavie, who had also been sick in the previous months [*JSA*]. Because of yellow fever and other travel catastrophes, Philippine and Miss Pratte did not return from the south until November 30, necessitating a juggling of responsibilities at St. Ferdinand during her long absence. Some of them landed on Lucile.

A few months later, June 2-5, 1823, the long-awaited Jesuits arrived from Maryland to found their seminary a few miles away: Fathers Felix Van Quickenborne and Pierre Joseph Timmermans,[21] two lay brothers, Henri and Peter, and seven novices, recruited mostly in Belgium, along with three enslaved couples from Maryland: Tom, Moses, Isaac, Polly, Nancy, and Succy.[22] Among the novices were Pierre De Smet, who would later become the celebrated missionary to the West, and Peter Verhaegen, who would be instrumental in the foundation of

---

21 Felix Van Quickenborne, SJ (1788-1837), made vows in Ghent, Belgium, and came as master of novices to Georgetown, then as superior of the new foundation in Missouri in 1823. He had various relationships with the Society of the Sacred Heart, including a troubled one with Philippine in Florissant. Pierre Timmermans, SJ (1788-1824), was born in Belgium, ordained in 1820, and missioned to Missouri in 1823.
22 Kelly Schmidt, "Enslaved Faith Communities," 49 and unpublished list.

St. Louis University and a trusted friend of Philippine in her old age.[23]

Lucile's first encounter with slavery was closer to home. Sometime around 1822, Eliza Nebbit was given to Mother Duchesne by Bishop Dubourg. Eliza was probably born about 1810 in Kentucky. While Society tradition turned her into an abandoned orphan, in fact she had family that had also been brought to Missouri from Kentucky. She then lived with the community in Florissant until she went, presumably in 1825, to Louisiana to take part in the new foundation at Saint Michael, where she spent the rest of her life, dying there in 1889. In 1826, another enslaved woman, Rachel, arrived in the Sacred Heart community in Florissant. Rachel had belonged to Bishop Dubourg until he left for France and resigned his episcopacy in Upper Louisiana; then she served in the household of priests connected to the college in Saint Louis, before being transferred to Philippine the same year. Her behavior with the priests had been difficult, and apparently, it continued to be so; in the end she was sold in 1829, leaving behind no further record. Both Eliza and Rachel would therefore have been known to Lucile during the years she lived at Florissant.

A few months after Lucile had arrived on April 15, 1822, Saint Ferdinand in Florissant saw its first ceremony of religious vows in the Society of the Sacred Heart in Missouri, when Emilie Saint-Cyr, who had previously been a boarding student there, made her first vows on July 16.[24] Others were entering the

---

[23] Peter Verhaegen (1800-1868) was president of St. Louis University, then leader of the Jesuit mission in Kansas, a friend of Philippine and pastor in St. Charles at the time of death. He was later again professor at the university, then again in St. Charles, where he died.

[24] It was not the first time in America: already in 1822, Anna Xavier Murphy had made her final profession on May 14, and Mary Layton her first vows on June 6, both in Grand Coteau, Louisiana.

Society and the community was growing. The year 1825 saw several important transitions in the religious community of which Lucile was a part. On April 17, Mary Ann O'Connor made her first vows, along with the two Hamilton sisters, Mathilde Xavier and Eulalie Regis. Mary Ann O'Connor would in years to come be Lucile's faithful companion and support in the Indian mission, where like Lucile, she died and was buried.

Meanwhile, Mary Ann O'Connor had other moves to make before the Potawatomi mission in 1841. She accompanied Philippine to the new foundation in St. Louis, the "City House," on May 2, 1827, along with one of the orphans being cared for at Florissant, Mary Knapp, who would later enter the Society. A few years later, Mary Ann O'Connor would join Lucile in the refounded house at St. Charles.

It had been Philippine's dream in coming to the United States to spend the rest of her life in service to the indigenous people. As we know, she was led to think it was to them that she was coming. Instead, most of her life on the frontier was spent with children of French colonials and increasingly, of Americans from the East.[25] In 1824, she had the chance to establish a small school for a few Indian girls at Florissant, when the Jesuits had begun such a school for boys and Father Van Quickenborne brought a few girls to her. A room was prepared for them near the free day school that the religious were already operating, and Lucile was put in charge of them. She reveled in the charge, feeling that her dreams were being fulfilled, until one of the girls fell ill. Lucile nursed the girl with every possible effort, but the girl died nevertheless. Lucile had a great fear of corpses, and was

---

25 In a letter to Elisabeth Galitzine, Jan. 7, 1841, arguing for the Sugar Creek mission, she wrote: "When we came here under the wing of Bishop Dubourg, we all thought that we would work for the Indians, and he himself let us hope so....We have been deceived here, at least I have, all of whose attractions and wishes went toward them."

unable to look at the girl after death, a fear that she carried all her life [*AL* 1877, p. 273]. This may be why after that year, the Indian girls were put into the charge of Mary Ann O'Connor. Nevertheless, Lucile wrote to Mother Barat in May 1827 that "I have no other pleasure than that of being in the midst of my little Indians to teach them the catechism." The school continued until about 1832, though both Lucile and Mary Ann O'Connor had left Florissant. By that time, however, the tribes had been forced farther West, and they were not willing to leave their children so far away. The Indian school did not continue at Florissant.

In her usual way, Philippine in her capacity of superior could be critical of her sisters and complimentary at the same time. She reported to Mother Barat that Lucile "lacks firmness and does not hold the day students well." She is always willing to praise them. Nor does she, in Philippine's estimation, understand a word of English, "something really necessary for the leader because one is often obliged to make use of those of lower rank for that language," that is, a younger religious or a novice. Philippine certainly knew this because she herself had to do it. Nevertheless, she admitted that Lucile was well liked: "Mother Lucile has won the hearts of all in the house and in the day school. Everyone admires her devotedness and her other virtues, especially Mother Octavie." Lucile was a good administrator who knew how to run a house.[26] That was a skill that she would need in coming years.

Even as Philippine herself fretted about her inability to be with the Indians, so too did Lucile, who wrote to Mother Barat on September 6, 1827: "All I want is to do God's will and end my days among the Indians. The Jesuits are going to the Osage in the

---

26  Letters from Philippine Duchesne to Madeleine Sophie Barat, June 24, Sept 1, 1824.

spring, and I asked if they would build us a house. They promised, but not now because the Indians would think the black robes have wives. I want to be so good that when you send one of us to the savages, you will put me with this number."

# SUPERIOR AT ST. CHARLES (1828-1841)

The first foundation in St. Charles, in September 1818, had been abandoned after one year in favor of Florissant on the east side of the Missouri, but the closure had never been absolute. Throughout the next years, there were efforts to get the Sacred Heart back to St. Charles, now joined by the Jesuits, who already at their arrival in the area had begun a ministry there. There was already a simple wooden church in a different location than the earlier one on Jackson Street, the second one in the town, dating to about 1792. By January 1825, the Jesuits had committed to setting up a parish and building a new church. On March 1 of that year, they purchased the Duquette house in which the religious had spent their one year there, as well as land for a church nearby. Newly ordained Father Verhaegen was put in charge of the project [Garraghan 1.203-211]. The house, built in 1794, was twenty-five by thirty-five feet, with five feet of gallery all around. With that commitment made, the Religious of the Sacred Heart determined to return, once the parish church had been built and the Jesuits were established in it.

At the same time, Eugenie Audé in Louisiana was planning a new establishment at St. Michael, on the Mississippi River closer to New Orleans, and Philippine was planning the new house in St. Louis. Who would be superior of the two new houses? Lucile and Octavie Berthold were obvious candidates, along with Anna Xavier Murphy at Grand Coteau. Philippine knew that Lucile was aware of the possibility, but she dismissed the idea of sending Lucile south: "I do not think that she could sustain that trial, especially since the arrival of the fathers (Jesuits) here; and in spite of our poverty, she is very happy. After Mother Eugenie, she would be judged poorly by the parents, who appreciate Mother Anna, and so do the children." Father Van Quickenborne was going frequently to St. Charles, and the Jesuits were planning their return. "In time that will be the right place for Mother Lucile, whom the father appreciates greatly. She is the only one he would like to see as superior, even in Saint Louis, so greatly does he fear for others the unhealthy atmosphere there" (Philippine to Madeleine Sophie Barat, January 6, 1825).

In spite of such glowing words about Lucile, Philippine dismissed the possibility not only of her as superior in the south but also at the new foundation in St. Louis: "It is often said of her: not much ability, but a good person." Nevertheless, at Florissant, there were more than thirty boarders, orphans, and Indian girls in three separate groups.[27] Lucile was mistress general of the orphans and day students, mistress of choir, and assistant treasurer. Such contradictions in Philippine's assessment of persons were typical. She was critical of others who did not match her ideals of behavior and character. Anna Xavier Murphy, already at Grand Coteau, was chosen to lead that house while Eugenie Audé went to the new foundation at St. Michael. Philippine herself would go to the City House in St. Louis, leaving St. Ferdinand in the hands of Octavie Berthold, and Lucile would lead the refoundation in St. Charles. By 1830, however, Octavie was at the City House, already showing signs of the

---

27 Letters Philippine to Madeleine Sophie Barat, January 6, 1825; May 13, 1827.

cancer that would take her life in 1833 at the age of forty-six. Catherine Thiéfry, who had come from Europe the year before, had taken charge at St. Ferdinand in Florissant.

Philippine departed Florissant for the new house in St. Louis on May 2, 1827, but there would be yet another year before the return to St. Charles could be carried out. Philippine again gave Mother Barat her assessment of Lucile's ability to govern, on October 7, 1827, saying that she was the least satisfactory, compared to Octavie Berthold, newly professed local Regis Hamilton, and recently arrived Hélène Dutour. Lucile was not very regular—a solid French religious virtue. "My absence (to the City House) does not worry her; she is better following her own style. She has long been accustomed to meddle in many things and to be always on the move." In retrospect, Lucile's freedom of style and movement may have been characteristics that later enabled her to thrive among the Indians, whose customs differed immensely from those of Europeans.

On June 25, 1828, Philippine set out with Bishop Rosati and Father Van Quickenborne for St. Charles on an inspection tour of the house that she had left nine years earlier. They returned to St. Louis two days later. Philippine did not record in her journal her impressions of the site, which had been unoccupied during the intervening time. The founders set out for St. Charles on October 10, 1828: Mothers Duchesne, Octavie, Lucile, and Mary Ann O'Connor. Philippine noted in her journal that a pretty stone church had been built to replace the old wooden one that had fallen into ruin. This time she noted that the house where they had lived for a year some ten years ago, was also "in bad condition," a severe underestimation compared to Lucile's later details. Nevertheless, in the largest room, they set up an altar, and on the evening of October 11, they packed in

"Bishop Rosati, eight Jesuits, two Lazarists, and two seminarians" along with the four religious, to sing Matins and Lauds and lay the cornerstone of the altar with the relic of St. Adeodatus.[28] For the occasion, the house accounts record gifts received from the houses of St. Louis ($60), St. Ferdinand ($60), and Lafourche, Louisiana ($50). On the next day, the solemn consecration of the parish church took place, with Mass, Vespers, and Benediction [*JSA* 10.10-12.1828].

After a few days, Mothers Duchesne and Octavie returned across the river, leaving Lucile and Mary Ann in the new foundation with $40. The chaplain's fee was fixed at $100 annually [*JSA* 10.25.1828]. They began to feel the isolation of being so far from everyone else. The Jesuits next door, Fathers Verreydt and Smedts, tried to help as much as they could. They sent a cow and calf, and regular supplies of vegetables. They had a garden and an orchard with a hundred apple and six plum trees. Lucile planted peach and pear trees, which must have been brought from St. Louis. She loved to describe fruits and vegetables that France did not have, like the sweet potatoes (*patates douces*) and watermelons. From the front porch, they had a lovely view of the Missouri River winding its way through forests. By rule, they were to keep silence except when speech was necessary. They tried, but started laughing all the time at some of the ridiculous things they were doing. The house contained six small rooms eight feet in length and five feet wide, with eight doors and two windows. Above was a little attic where one could not go without falling through. There were mice in the walls that nibbled their fingers and woke them in the morning.[29]

---

28  St. Adeodatus (570-618) was pope 615-618 CE, known for his charitable works.
29  As related to Mme Melanie Rambeau in a letter of February 21, 1831.

We moved into a house without window glass or frames, full of rats. I didn't even have a bed to sleep on; I gave mine to Mother Duchesne. I found an old church carpet, and rolled up in it, along with the Indian woman I brought from Florissant to cook. Holy House of Poverty. The vestry consists of 4 pairs of sheets, 6 napkins, 8 chemises, but still no armoire to put them in. I found one in the middle of the courtyard and had it brought in, and am arranging it and it serves as library, lingerie, and infirmary.

They wondered where to get a cat, and the next day, one showed up, moved in, and took possession of every hole. It cleared out the place and then disappeared. There was little furniture. They did their own carpentry and masonry to save money and made twelve benches, a table, and a chicken coop. There were holes in the floor so that falling into the space below was a danger. They were obliged to sleep rolled up in covers over the head: either suffocate or freeze.

They found the inhabitants good people, but poor. There were a few other larger towns in the surroundings. St. Charles was undergoing large population growth and was then at 14,000, with twenty families moving in each day, attracted by fertile soil and nearby lead mines. Protestants were the majority of the population and were not hostile to Catholics; in fact, after a while, several Protestant children in the school had permission to become Catholics.

There was a good orchard on the property, and as soon as they were able, they began vegetable gardening. The soil was fertile. There were also many examples of the generosity of neighbors. At one point, as winter approached, Lucile wondered where they would get firewood, for which they had no money.

Soon a neighbor drove up with a wagonload of wood, offering to bring more when needed. Another time, they had no corn for the cows and chickens, when a friend arrived with a big supply of corn, and at the same time a mother brought her daughter as a boarder and paid six months board in advance [Callan 233; Cahier 1.493-494].

They began the school in early November as a free school, but had sixteen, then quickly twenty, externs whose families could afford one gourde or five francs (about one dollar) a month.[30] No one, however, was turned away for inability to pay. "There is promise of boarders, but after winter, because the river separates them and parents fear the poverty and cold."[31] The Jesuits were also beginning a free boys' school and quickly had one hundred students. In January of the next year, 1829, Philippine could write to Bishop Rosati that Lucile was happy with her twenty-four students in St. Charles. In the fall, they were able to begin the boarding school, with a boarding fee of fifteen dollars a quarter, but again, no one was turned away for inability to pay.

The unnamed Indian woman who came with them from St. Louis to cook was still there on January 20, 1829. By this time, her role had expanded to ironing both for the religious and for the Jesuits. So well had the religious told her about Mother Barat in France that she professed her love for her, and Lucile asked Mother Barat for a little cross just for her.

Four months later, on March 15, 1829, Philippine returned for a visit, bringing with her reinforcement in the person of Mary Layton, who had recently returned from having been in Grand Coteau since its foundation in 1821. By that time, there were

---

30 Although the model they were used to was a paying boarding school and a free day school, or "poor school," it is important to note that from the beginning this third alternative, a paying day school, was evolving.
31 Lucile to Mother Barat and to Louis Barat on the same date, November 16, 1828.

thirty-six day students in St. Charles. Philippine stayed for a day and a half to observe and encourage the little band on the other side of the Missouri. Philippine was there again in April 1830 with Catherine Thiéfry, who had arrived from France the previous June, along with two others, Felicity Lavy-Brun and Julie Bazire [*JSA*], but as visitors. Although Lucile had understood that there would be reinforcements soon and begged for one of the new missionaries for St. Charles, none was forthcoming, though Mother Barat was keenly aware of their need. She promised in her letter of June 26, 1829, to send material resources regularly, so that "in a few years, your sacristy will have everything that a Sacred Heart house should have." They remained only three in St. Charles. As in the first years of the first group in 1818, the close quarters and necessary mixing of roles rendered distinctions between choir and coadjutrix in the community meaningless. Later, the same would be true in the beginnings in Kansas. Here in St. Charles, Lucile became accustomed to a simpler community life that would prepare her to replicate it as superior at Sugar Creek.

On September 4, 1829, many of the religious from across the Missouri must have been present in St. Charles for the celebration of the final vows of Mary Ann O'Connor.[32] Though they could not have known it then, she and Lucile would in their later years be loyal support to each other and some of the longest lasting members of the Kansas mission. Another few months brought returning Philippine and visiting Mother Thiéfry. According to Lucile's letter to Mother Barat April 25, 1830, they were charmed by the children, the location, and the view. The building was still fragile: it leaked in rain, the founda-

---

32 *JSA* 9.4.1829, where the correction is made that it was mistakenly first recorded in August.

tion was crumbling, and the roof had to be held up with added beams. Philippine came again on July 4, 1830, to visit Lucile, who was sick, as was Mary Layton. She was accompanied this time by Susannah McKay, who visited her sick mother on the way [*JSA*].[33]

Lucile had been begging for more help for the growing school, and sometime in 1831, a novice, Sr. Aubuchon, was sent there to help, but she proved to be no help at all. On July 29, 1831, Philippine came to St. Charles at the community's request to get her, since she had been having "frightening crises" while there. Philippine's journal reports for that day that, brought back to St. Louis, she was better now and they wanted to keep her. At some later date within a few months, she returned to St. Charles, the crises resumed, and on September 8, Lucile took her to back to St. Louis, from where she returned to her family [*JSA*].

On August 1, 1831, Philippine reported to Mother Barat on her most recent visit to St. Charles, that of July 29. It is an interesting contrast in perceptions. A few months earlier, in April 1830, Lucile had written to Mother Barat that Mother Duchesne and Mother Thiéfry were charmed by the children and the environment, and that Mother Duchesne "was edified by the good conduct of our children; not a single word in the class, even though that day we had to leave them alone for a few moments....," an expression of good European behavioral expectations. Now in the next year, Philippine again critiqued Lucile in her report to Mother Barat, as she had when they were both back in Florissant:

> I notice that everything there is badly regulated:

---

[33] Susannah Aloysia McKay (1802-1860) was born in New York, entered the Society at Florissant in 1825 and made her final profession in 1830, and died in St. Charles. It is not known when or why she and her mother came to Missouri earlier.

poor health, an easy-going temperament, a certain tendency to improvise, all indicate that the children are somewhat left to themselves and may develop serious faults of which we would be guilty if we do not attend to them....If [another who might come from France] is in charge, I am a little afraid that our male friends will not be pleased, and neither will the parents, who detest change. Maybe in second place with as much authority as possible and in charge of the little girls, she will be able to counterbalance the extreme weakness of the mother [Lucile] and the lack of discipline from which would follow complete disorder. I have given my advice, but it is considered quite impossible unless we let the poor lambs do as they like for part of the day.

Clearly, Lucile's manner of governing was freer in style than that expected by those from France and endorsed by Philippine. When later Philippine spent her year under Lucile as superior at Sugar Creek, it must have been quite a trial for both of them.

The house at St. Charles continued to be in need of more help. Reinforcements for the American mission arrived in May 1831: Marie Anne de Coppens, Henriette de Kersaint, Adèle de Toisonnier, and Louise Prudhomme. Mother Barat's accompanying letter to Lucile said that one of them—to be determined—was destined for St. Charles, but none came.[34] On July 27, 1832, Lucile complained to Mother Barat that the

---

34 The letter also stated that one of the new arrivals was a fervent and virtuous novice, having been in another order previously, but transferring in order to follow her call on the American mission. That would be Mary Anne de Coppens, who had previously been a Carmelite. She went to Louisiana, where she was unstable and unhappy. She returned to France in 1836 and died the next year.

foundation was "languishing." Finally, reliable help arrived in the person of Louisianian Eulalie Guillot, who remained until her death in 1839.[35]

About the same time, after a visit to St. Charles, Philippine wrote to Mother Barat on December 13, 1832, that she found Lucile in bad health, with constant pain and few children. Nevertheless, she conceded, "her house does much good through relationships with Protestants, or as they say here, different denominations who are seeking the truth. Her Irishwoman is prone to controversy." Knowing Philippine's ways of thinking based on her French Catholic conditioning, we can conclude that her remark is not complimentary. What controversy Mary Ann O'Connor was stirring up is unknown.

Some entries from the account books during these years can give some idea of daily life. There are regular purchases of feed for horses, meat, sugar, and flour. A reimbursement for Mother Duchesne's travel from St. Louis cost $6.50. In April 1831, they are still buying wood for heating, but they are also selling eggs from their chickens. They dug a well in 1838, with loans from Philippine of $30 and then $20 more.

By 1833 the number of students had increased, and the old building had deteriorated to such an extent that they needed to build. That spring, Father Van Quickenborne began collecting money from the parishioners, who responded generously on paper, but by summer an epidemic of cholera stopped progress on fundraising and building. School was closed, parents of many children died, and Lucile wrote to Bishop Rosati on August 7, 1833, that the convent had become a hospital, with only one religious, probably herself, able to care for the rest [Callan, 234].

---

35 Born in Lafourche, Louisiana, in 1811, she had briefly been with the Sisters of Loretto there, but entered the Society at St. Michael in 1828 and made her first vows there before going north, with final profession in St. Louis in 1834.

By October, it was not at all clear that they would have the funds. Nevertheless, Lucile invited Bishop Rosati to come inspect the site where they hoped to build in the spring. In November, Philippine returned to St Charles to see plans for the new building. Father Van Quickenborne, not always the easiest person to get along with, was pastor and continued to help raise the money. They began to build, and by March 1834 had raised 7500 francs in donations. Then came another cholera epidemic, which delayed construction. In November, Lucile wrote to Mother Barat that progress had been slightly delayed by the serious illness of the pastor, now recovered. Without going into debt, she wrote, they will have a roof on the new building before cold weather. They will have to beg for funds to complete the inside. The motherhouse promised 3.000 *livres* (now equivalent to francs) on loan that will be used when it comes. She has borrowed on that assurance. On July 24, 1835, Philippine was once again in St. Charles with $300 for the new house, part of a sale of jewelry from France, a gift of Father Barat.

By November 1835, according to Philippine, they were ready to move into their new brick house, "which is larger than the one here" (St. Ferdinand). In January 1836, they were still paying off the loan, and a gift of $200 from Mother Xavier Murphy at Grand Coteau was a big help. With the community and school now moved into their new house, Philippine wrote to a friend back in France that Mother Mathevon was now in "a pretty brick house where she could have 40 students, but the area is not producing them. There are only farmers who have little money."[36] The school list for 1835 gives thirteen boarders and sixty day students. Probably the number forty is the large number of boarders that they could now have in their new space.

---

36  To Angelique Lavauden, December 20, 1835.

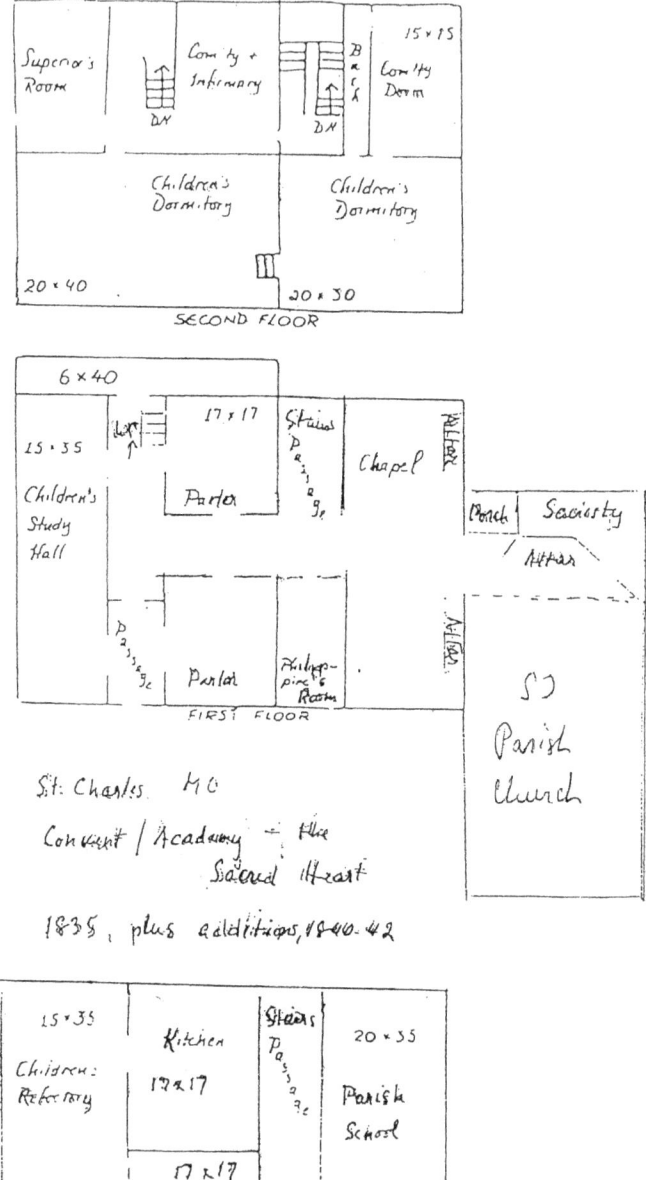

Floor plan, 1835 and 1840 buildings. Unknown provenance.

St. Charles, 1835 and 1840 buildings

In 1834, during the course of construction of the new building, Father Van Quickenborne proposed a new direction that would have changed the whole nature of the school. On September 7 of that year, he wrote to Bishop Rosati about the request of a parish priest in Natchitoches, Louisiana, suggesting that the Sacred Heart school in St. Charles become a residential school for *filles de couleur* from Louisiana, by which, it is clear from the letter, he meant mulattos. By the time he wrote about it to Rosati, he had already discussed the proposal with Mother Mathevon, who, he writes, was eager to pursue the possibility. Of course, he adds, there could then be no question of white students in the boarding school, though the day school could continue as it was.

> I take the liberty of proposing the question to your Lordship: would it be prudent to receive them and shall the offer be accepted? Madame Lucille[37] desires nothing better. Madame Eugénie [Audé], when she was here, gave her approval (but she made no definite arrangements as regards St Charles). Madame Lucille assures me that Madame Barat will send some subjects and a little money. If the colored girls come, there will be no question of getting any white girls. The house would be exclusively for the former. However, the school for day pupils could be kept up separately.[38]

The offer was not accepted, the change did not happen, probably because the bishop or Mother Barat or both did not approve. Sources of income would have been unclear.

By 1836, there was need for more service help. Slavery was widespread in the St. Louis area, and the Jesuits in Florissant engaged a number of enslaved workers on their farm. A letter of Mother Barat to Lucile Mathevon, dated September 2, 1836, says:

> First of all, it's about a Negro whom you seem to need and whom you ask to purchase. If your finances permit you, I am willing, since you have so little help and I can see that you would want it.[39]

---

37  Occasionally her name appears in sources with the more usual spelling, but generally the spelling is with one l.
38  Translation by Garraghan, 1.215-16.
39  *D'abord c'est pour un nègre dont vous paroissez avoir besoin et que vous demandez à*

This transaction seems never to have taken place. However, one month later, rental of services of, or agreement with, a Black woman for work appears in the house accounts:

| October 1836 | louage de la négresse | 3.50 |
| November 1836 | Robe pour la négresse | 3.00 |
| September 1837 | paiement de la négresse | 21.00 |
| November 1837 | gage de la négresse de payment | 21.00 |
| July 1838 | gage de Thérèse négresse | 12.00 |
| October 1838 | gage de la négresse | 75.00 |
| October 1839 | gage de la négresse | 75.00 |

The legal status of this woman is ambiguous. She could have been rented from another slaveholder or she could have been a free laborer, or even if enslaved, doing extra work for pay, which was often done. *Louage* can mean rental or contract; *gage* is more likely wage. In November 1836, instead of payment, a dress was purchased for her, which suggests that she was recipient of the payments. The amounts into 1837 and 1838 are substantial, indicating regular work of an unspecified kind, but she does not seem to be resident at the convent. The 1840 census lists no persons of color, enslaved or free, at the convent. There are no similar entries for services in the next years until 1852, then specifically for laundry work.

Once the school had been established in the new 1835 building, it was just a short distance to the parish church, but the religious felt the absence of their own chapel. By 1838, they were planning an extension of the 1835 building, just twenty-five feet more, that would create an inside space for a chapel to be used by

---

*achetter. Si vos finances vous le permettent, je le veux bien ayant si peu de secours je conçois que vous deviez le desirer.*

religious and students, connected by wall with the Jesuit church, with an opening into its sanctuary. Permissions were easily obtained, and the construction was financed by gifts from the motherhouse, St. Michael, and Lucile's family in France. Bishop Rosati blessed the chapel in the spring of 1840 on his final visit to St. Charles [Callan 237]. This extension greatly added to available inside space. Besides the chapel on the ground floor, it provided for a larger children's dormitory above and eventually the parish school below.

When Eugenie Audé was named assistant general in 1833, she was first tasked with a visit to all the American houses, which must have included St. Charles. A report on that visit is not extant. The second official visit from a representative of the superior general was that of Elisabeth Galitzine in October 1840.[40] She had come to America in the capacity of provincial according to the new government structure that had been approved by a general council the year before. She left 146 recommendations for the church, refectory, kitchen, pantry, vestry, dormitory, classes, library, treasury, garden, boarding school, and twenty-seven personally for Lucile as superior. Among them was a directive to make her will, in favor of three other RSCJ in the St. Louis area.[41] Another was to begin a house journal, which had not been done from 1828; it was begun in early 1841. Some of the others had to do with her role in the spiritual guidance of the community and the students, and the erection of the sodalities already traditional in Sacred Heart schools. Postulants could be admitted in the local house, first in the category of retreatants,

---

40 Elisabeth Galitzine, RSCJ (1795-1843), an elite convert from Russian Orthodoxy, came as assistant general to America in 1840 and again in 1843. She was instrumental especially in the foundations in Kansas and New York. She died of yellow fever at St. Michael during her second visit.
41 This was normal procedure, since the convents were not incorporated, so the properties were held in the name of the superior.

then postulants, not to be sent immediately to the novitiate in Florissant, but evaluated locally. If satisfactory, they should be sent to Florissant a little time before their reception of the habit and entry into the novitiate. Already Lucile was getting a dose of the multiple rules that were being created for daily life in the Society and that she as superior was responsible to enforce. We will see later at St. Mary's that enforcement of rules was not Lucile's strong suit.

During Lucile's years in St. Charles, besides her co-founder Mary Ann O'Connor and Eulalie Guillot, already mentioned, a series of others came and went. Mary Layton, one of the founders at Grand Coteau, returned to Missouri and spent some months there in 1829. Later, she would join Lucile at St. Mary's.[42] Others in St. Charles for part of the time were Americans Ann Egerty and Maria Knapp, and Irish-born Aloysia McKay and Catherine Redmond. The number of boarders between 1828 and 1836 averaged eleven or twelve, and day students forty to sixty. With the completion of the new building in 1835, the numbers of boarders increased to twenty-five and more. The Jesuits continued to staff the parish and maintain cordial and helpful relations. Pastors in those years after Felix Van Quicknborne were Judochus Van Assche, SJ, and Christian Hoecken, SJ, in 1836, and Jan Smedts, SJ, 1837 to 1843. By that time, Lucile had long left St. Charles to answer the call of the frontier.

---

42 The name of the mission located there 1848, is St. Mary's. The name of the later town from the 1860s is St. Marys, Kansas (no apostrophe).

# JOURNEY TO THE POTAWATOMI MISSION AT SUGAR CREEK (JULY 1841)

The mission project had been long planned with the cooperation of Elisabeth Galitzine in her capacity as provincial of the American houses. The Potawatomi had arrived in Kansas on the Trail of Death in 1838, and the Jesuit mission and boys' school established since July 1840. There were many others, mostly Methodist and Baptist, but all had been abandoned by 1842. Thus, during the first year that the Religious of the Sacred Heart joined the mission, Sugar Creek was the only one operating in the area [Garraghan 2.202-203; Chicoine 24-35].

Lucile had gone to the City House in St. Louis in advance to prepare for the departure. According to Lucile's own account, Mother Galitzine had given her consent but was fearful and wanted to delay departure. But Father Verhaegen would have none of it. Between Providence and himself, he was confident that everything would go well.

> We had to go get Mother [Mary Ann] O'Connor at St. Charles. There Mother [Regis] Hamilton wanted to oppose her departure and told him, I have no one to replace her. But [he] cut her short and said this is not my business, prepare everything. That dear mother did not dare say another word and he brought her to St. Louis. So there we were all

together. I prepared the packets and purchased our little *ménage*: marmite, stove for warmth, pot, coffee maker, and provisions of sugar, coffee, rice, molasses, crackers, flour, stove for cooking, utensils for working the ground and the carpentry, in sum, everything needed in a region where one finds little to buy of these sorts of things.

By the time of departure, the mission included three religious: Lucile, Mary Ann O'Connor, and Louise Amiot.[43] There seems to be some ambiguity about how it was finally decided that Philippine would also go. Though the usual story credits Father Peter Verhaegen, as touchingly told by Callan [p. 635], he in fact had written to Bishop Rosati on December 16, 1840, that though Mother Galitzine wanted Philippine to go, he did not think it wise to bring that *vieille femme*. Perhaps he changed his mind in the following months. On March 10, 1841, Mother Provincial Elisabeth Galitzine wrote to Jesuit Provincial Pierre De Smet that she had deliberated and decided to go ahead with the mission, desired by Mother Barat. She could send Julie Bazire, former superior at Grand Coteau, Lucile Mathevon from St. Charles, and Mother Duchesne, only those three: "I can do no more." Sometime in the next few months, the list changed to Lucile, Mary Ann O'Connor, and Louise Amiot.

In a letter to Mother Barat, May 10, 1841, Lucile writes of preparations for the journey and sounds as if Philippine is resigned to not going for reasons of health. Lucile, at least, wants

---

43 Other spellings of her name include Amiote, Amiotte, and Amyote. Born in Canada in 1818, she entered the Society in St. Louis, and must have come from a fur trading family, for both Philippine and Lucile wrote of her that she had already lived among the Indians and knew their language (Philippine to Galitzine, 1.25.1841; Chicoine 34-35).

to believe it: "Our good Mother Duchesne is content. She only asked to go because she saw that Mother O'Connor and I were chosen. She is satisfied....She is diminishing; I doubt she could go far." Given Philippine's lifelong desires, one greatly doubts that she was as content as Lucile imagines. Yet go she did, apparently in the end with Verhaegen as the one who insisted that she go, if not to do anything, then to pray. Callan's narrative attributes this to one of Lucile's accounts of the foundation, but in fact, it appears only in her letter to Mother Barat of August 3, 1841, a few weeks after their arrival at Sugar Creek.

The author of Lucile's notice in the *Annual Letters* describes the consternation of the inhabitants of St. Charles at the loss of Mother Mathevon, blaming Mother Galitzine for taking her away and wishing that she had never come to America—a sentiment shared with many others for other reasons. Though the actual departure was not until June 29, Lucile had been abruptly pulled from St. Charles some months earlier by Father Verhaegen. There were four religious: Lucile as superior, Mary Ann O'Connor, Louise Amiot, and of course, Philippine Duchesne, who was reluctantly included. Besides Verhaegen, their fellow travelers included Fathers Jan Smedts, SJ, and Renaud[44] from the cathedral, and the enslaved man Edmund, who had been at the City House from at least 1834. A large group accompanied them, "five or six gentlemen and a dozen ladies," to the steamboat, which they boarded on July 2.[45] Lucile names Bishop Lachanse [Chanche, SS] of Natchez, Father Vandevelde,

---

44 Renaud is the third name in one account; in the other, it is Lecuillier. Joseph Renaud, a diocesan priest, was an episcopal vicar, official representative. That may explain his membership in the group.
45 This to Mother Galitzine from Westport, July 4 (probably 5), 1841. Lucile's account does not say where they boarded the steamboat, but it was likely St. Charles on the Missouri River. It was unlikely to have been St. Louis on the Mississippi, which would require extra time to reach the Missouri to the north.

SJ, president of St. Louis University, "Misters Kelly, benefactor of the establishment, Mr. Borne Demies Fortune Wolche, ... Mrs. McLaughlin, Amon Wolche, and the Misses Murphy Fortune McKeys, all benefactors of this establishment." The bishop had arrived in St. Louis the day before and came along to give them an apostolic blessing. They were well treated by Captain Cuser and his wife, who expressed interest in Catholic instruction. In the first three days of the voyage, they were amazed at the number of towns that had been built up along the Missouri River. Some had Catholics but no church and no priest. Mother Duchesne looked as if she had regained her youth, walking up and down the decks in a way she had not previously been able to do.

Their third day on the steamboat was July 4, which was duly celebrated in the afternoon. A solemn group of about fifty men sat silently in rows, the women elsewhere. Father Verhaegen delivered "a sermon appropriate for the solemnity of the day," to which they applauded "in the American style with hands and feet." White wine and other liquor were then served. They all partook of the iced sherry that was offered. The priests joined the men in general merriment, complete with tambourine and clarinet.

They disembarked five miles from Westport to spend the night at the home of a Mrs. Chouteau, where on Sunday they were able to have Mass. Two horse-drawn *Waigaines* arrived from Westport for their baggage, and they spent the next night there with a family who gave them a good dinner. The following night they camped out at a beautiful river and had a supper of coffee and ham under the trees. Instead of sleeping, reports Lucile, Father Verhaegen talked all night and kept them awake. The drivers, however, slept too soundly, so that two of the horses had gotten loose and were not to be found. Catching them again took the first half of the next day, which set them back from their travel schedule. This obliged them to spend two more nights camping out on the prairie. Lucile claimed to have enjoyed it.

Finally, when they had reached the twenty-first mile, Father Aelen came to meet them from the Sugar Creek settlement to lead them to their last night out, at a trading post on the Osage River run by a Frenchman, Mr. Girou, who received them graciously and even gave them his bed. The story of their arrival has often been told. Lucile herself described it several times. The next day, two mounted Indians came to meet them every two or three miles. At one mile from the village,

> [W]e found the whole village in procession that came in front of us, arranged in perfect order, the 2 fathers Aelen and Eysvogels on horseback with their square hats, the chief of the Indians, 2 children carrying two flags, one white with a red cross and stars, the other red. All were on horseback. Following were 150 mounted Indians in their best dress, the horses well harnessed. After, about 300 men with rifles followed, then the men on foot, the women, girls, and boys. There were 6 flags, all in the best order. For our welcome, 2 Indians took the bridles of our horses and held them this way during the discharge of rifles. Then the cavalry lined up on both sides of our wagons and they advanced our wagons this way through the middle of the cavalry, then they made semi-circles around us, then half crescents in perfect order. Not a single horse's foot advanced farther than another. The women said their rosary. When we arrived near the house of Reverend Father

Aelen, they had us get down from the wagon and sit on prepared benches. 5 Jesuit fathers, 4 Religious of the Sacred Heart, all the Indians arranged in 4 lines around us in the most perfect order. Then the chief approached us and greeted us. What happiness for us, we see these religious arrive to instruct our children in the true religion. It was all resaid to us by the interpreter [Mathevon, *Journal of the Foundation*].

Then the chief's wife greeted them, followed by all the girls to shake their hands. Two girls presented to Mother Duchesne an image of the Sacred Heart of Jesus and of Mary, and Father Verhaegen told them that he had never seen such a reception. He introduced Philippine as "a lady of 73 who has wanted to come for 30 years to instruct the Indians, that she was filled with joy to see her desires accomplished." After a visit to the church, the religious were taken to the house of Mr. Bertrand, a leader of the village, and his American wife from Michigan. "It was a Friday. For the first time in my life, I ate meat on Friday out of obedience to Reverend Father Verhaegen, who gave the permission, taking the place of the bishop, and in a country where one does not find everything."

They were surprised to learn that their house was not ready, but they were temporarily given the house of an Indian, "a log house 18 feet long and 12 wide....situated below the church, in a pretty place. We were surrounded by Indians, but great people who sing continually the praise of God." There they stayed from July to October, the four of them crowded into this small space where they would live and conduct their classes. There were no locked doors, and the Indians would come in, sit down, and observe without speaking whenever they wanted, and eventually get up and leave. The religious learned not to be surprised or annoyed but simply to go on with what they were doing.

To Mother Galitzine, Lucile wrote the next month, that the Indians call them priestesses, not having a word in their language for religious. In the settlement were four French families, two Americans, and the rest Indians, of whom about 1,000 were Catholics while another 2,000 were not.

# LIFE AT SUGAR CREEK
# (1841-1848)

Immediately the missionaries set out to learn the Potawatomi language. Lucile reported that they had two Indian women as their teachers. Louise Amiot already had some knowledge of the language from earlier encounters. Lucile was musically talented, picked up the language fairly quickly, and was soon composing songs in Potawatomi. She reported that the Indians sang the Gloria and Credo of the Mass in Latin, but Vespers in their own language. She taught the women the litany of the Blessed Virgin for Sundays after Vespers [Lucile to E. Galtizine September 1841].

Within two weeks, they could read and sing in the Potawatomi language, though they did not yet know enough to speak. This progress report on their linguistic abilities did not fully apply to Philippine, who had never been good at foreign language, but she nevertheless tried. In a letter to her brother Hippolyte on September 12, she wrote out the *Gloria Patri* in Potawatomi, as well as eleven other vocabulary word equivalents, an indication of her careful study.

There is clear evidence that Lucile and perhaps the others did not want Philippine there, because she needed care; they feared they could not take care of her and that they would be blamed if she grew ill or died. As for Philippine, she would have liked nothing better than to die there. In Lucile's letter to Mother Barat of

August 3, 1841, she credits Father Verhaegen with the decision to bring Philippine, as he believed he was following the desire of Mother Galitzine, who believed it was Mother Barat's wish. But, Lucile wrote, she would be able only to suffer and pray.

Sugar Creek, Kansas, sign at place of first community.
Photo: Donna Collins

> She has aged a great deal in two years, her head is weakened, and she has a number of infirmities. We fear a health crisis. We cannot understand how the good Father could decide for her to take on such a voyage; but full of confidence in God, he always answered our objections with "even if she cannot work, she will pray for our missions; let us allow her to go there to die."[46]

Lucile goes on to say that Mother Duchesne prays all day and can do almost nothing but knit, which she does a great part of the day on her bed. The others suffer not being able to care for her as they would like. This is an interesting contrast to Lucile's account of the mission, where Philippine spent most of her day in the chapel, while the Indians called her "the woman who is always praying."[47] There, she was attempting a straightforward account and echoed her veneration of Mother Duchesne. Here she is making the argument that Philippine cannot stay.

Philippine was aware of this, but had a very different self-perception. In a letter to Mother Barat a few months later, February 28, 1842,

> They say that in the Rockies they live to be a hundred. As my health has been restored, and being only seventy-three, I think I would have at least ten more years of work. In earlier times, I believed that it was more perfect to wait for events to decide my fate.

---

46  Lucile to Mother Barat, August 3, 1841.
47  This title given to Philippine by the Potawatomi and reported by Lucile, was given only in French in her letter. The Potawatomi term, *Quah-kah-ka-num-ad*, was reconstructed in 1946 at the request of Louise Callan.

You see, Reverend Mother, if you wish to authorize me to go elsewhere, if I am *wanted*; and that is still very doubtful, for here I am only a burden with no occupation; moreover, they do not trust me and without doubt would be glad to see me leave. I realized from the first days that they wanted me elsewhere.

Mother Elisabeth Galitzine came for an official visit on March 19, 1842, and Bishop Kenrick from St. Louis in June. Both agreed and wrote to Mother Barat that Philippine should not stay. Mother Barat's reply to Lucile of April 16, after a report from Mother Galitzine, must have been reassuring to Lucile, even as it would have been devastating to Philippine:

> I see that it would be wiser for Mother Duchesne to return to St. Charles or wherever, according to her choice. I will try to make the decision with her.[48] Poor mother! What courage she has at her age, but it is too much. There is nothing more left for her now than retirement.

Philippine left July 24, no doubt to the great relief of the rest of the community, accompanied by Father Verhaegen, who escorted her back to St. Charles, where she would live another ten years. In her journal of events at Sugar Creek in the first years, Lucile notes Philippine's departure matter-of-factly, hiding her relief in formal reporting.

Another revelation in Lucile's letter to Mother Barat of

---

48 This letter is not extant. The next surviving letter from Mother Barat to Philippine is the one brought directly from Paris by Amelie Jouve in 1847.

August 3, 1841, is her reflection that God arranged it all to get them there, in spite of the fact that none had offered for that particular mission, except of course Philippine. However, fourteen years ago, Lucile confides, Father Van Quickenborne in St. Charles allowed her to make a vow for the mission to the Indians, with permission of her superiors. Those superiors would have been Philippine and Madeleine Sophie Barat. Just as Philippine had made a vow many years earlier in France to evangelize the Indians of America, so Lucile had made a similar vow while she was living in St. Charles.

The day school for Potawatomi girls was going well. Some Catholic families from nearby Osage tribes wanted the religious to establish a boarding school so that their daughters could go there. In her letter to Mother Barat of February 5, 1842, Lucile asked permission to do this. Mother Barat quickly replied on April 16 that surely, yes, they could do so, but where would they get the money? How much, she asks, would it cost for example, for ten *Osagettes*? Let her know, and they will begin in Paris to collect the money. This project was never undertaken.

Already a theme is beginning that will continue throughout the years of Lucile's leadership at the mission, sparked no doubt by reports from others sent to the motherhouse. Since the situation is so unstructured, Mother Barat encourages her to be more religious rather than less, to observe cloister, silence, and other religious observances as afar as possible. In addition, she adds,

> Be moderate in your efforts because you are no longer in the strength of your youth [she was 49], and strength fails all of a sudden when one works too much....I am told that you go out into the fields to show your Indians how to plant potatoes or other

vegetables. Couldn't your *nègre* [Edmund] do that service and you stay home? In your enclosure, all right, but going out could harm the rest. I rely on your guides [the Jesuits]. In doubtful cases ask their counsel and do it, for I know they are wise and prudent. If they agree about Mother Duchesne, they could advise her to return, for example, her confessor could demonstrate that it is necessary.

Meanwhile, Edmund, the enslaved man brought with them from St. Louis, was thriving.

Our Negro is most useful to us here. He is a man of importance. He is almost as respected as we are. He teaches the Indians carpentry. They are naturally skillful and easily imitate what they are shown to do. They made a pretty fence around the cemetery, but they did not know how to find the place for the gate. Edmund delivered them from the problem and helped them finish this little project. I am careful not to tell him that he is free here, for, though he is happy and perhaps too devoted to abuse it, it is nevertheless more sure if possible to leave him in his ignorance The Indians are almost as black as he, gentle by nature, and they all dress very decently.[49]

---

49 Lucile to Elisabeth Galitzine, August 1841. It is difficult to think that he did not know that Kansas was a free state, though the controversies about it did not irrupt until the 1850s. Edmund's last known appearance was on January 1, 1843, when the house journal reported that he returned from a trip into Westport with the news of the death of Mother Galitzine of yellow fever the previous month at St. Michael. The house journal reports that he read it in the newspaper, indication that Edmund was literate. He then disappears from the records.

The girls' school opened in mid-July 1841 at an estimated cost of six hundred dollars per year.[50] The numbers in attendance quickly rose to sixty—about forty regulars. Some would just disappear into the woods, where they would be discovered by one of the priests and brought back. There was also a small boarding school, and in one instance in very cold weather, three of the boarders escaped and made their way home, twenty or more miles away. Three weeks later, their parents brought them back with the request that they not be punished for their absence. The religious taught the girls basic literacy, as well as sewing, knitting and other needlecraft. They soon discovered that the Indian girls and women were quick learners and especially excelled at embroidery [Garraghan 2.208-210].

According to the house journal, the new house was built by the Indians in three days in March 1842, undoubtedly with direction from Edmund. The builders wanted no reward except a meal of pumpkin and beans cooked with lard. The house consisted of one large room with an attic accessible by ladder, which served as dormitory. The floor of the upper story consisted of loose boards that felt rather treacherous to walk on. The single room below had one corner designated as kitchen, another as community room, another as parlor, refectory, and storage. Class was sometimes held in a corner, though most of the time outside. Lucile relished the poverty of it all. Mother Galitzine intended to visit, then told them she could not because she was ordered back to Paris as fast as possible, but then she did find the time to spend two days. She was the first visitor in the new house, on March 19, 1842. She was there for Holy Week and was much impressed with the elaborate ceremonies at the church.

---

50 The estimated cost for the Jesuits and boys' school the same year, 1843, was $1800. The government paid only $300, none of which went to the Society.

Soon a government inspector, Mr. Mitchell, appeared in November for his first visit. He listened to the girls singing in English and Latin and was very satisfied. By this time, they had taken in a few boarders whose home was far away, though they did not yet have the capacity to operate a real boarding school. One was the *métis* daughter of a chief, who spoke Potawatomi, French, and English and was a valuable help as interpreter. At Mr. Mitchel's second visit in 1843, he was presented with moccasins and other needlework items made by the girls. He took their names and promised to show their work to Congress. Up to this time, the meager government allowance for the mission had gone mostly to the Jesuits, who had a larger operating budget. The RSCJ received nothing. The inspector promised the government would allot $500 for them. It was a long wait. Finally, in June 1845, the government approved, but payments did not arrive until January 11, 1846.[51] This happened only after the next inspector, Major Harvey, argued strenuously for support of the girls' mission school.

> The female school is conducted by five ladies of the society of the "Sacred Heart"; they have under their instruction between sixty and seventy girls. The progress of the girls is exceedingly flattering; they are taught the useful branches of female education; at the same time fashionable accomplishments are not neglected. A number of girls are supported and brought up in the family of the ladies. This school is supported entirely by these ladies and their friends [Garraghan 2.211].

---

51 House journal; Garragahn 2.210-213.

More help did arrive: the above report written October 8, 1844, speaks of five religious. Catherine Thiéfry had arrived to help on July 13, 1843, along with, according to the house journal, Xavier Cavanagh (or Cavenagh), otherwise unknown.[52] Mary Layton arrived a few months later, in early 1845, having been one of the founders at Grand Coteau, then for a few years in St. Charles. She would spend the rest of her life in the Kansas mission, until her death in 1876, just a few weeks after that of Lucile.

In the spring of 1844, flooding had cut off the mission from the surrounding area for weeks, until the water subsided. The Jesuit provincial then at St. Mary's on visit had to stay three weeks instead of three days. Lucile fills her letters with interesting descriptions; for example, in a letter to Julie Bazire in June 1846, she tells how they make lamps. They fill a white iron cup with wood, cotton, and lard. "It burns better than candles," she reports.

---

52  Or Kavanagh: see n. 96, p. 128.

# MOVE TO ST. MARY'S
# (1848)

From as early as 1844, the government wanted the tribes, promised their land in perpetuity only a few years before, to move farther west. In June 1846 at Council Bluffs, a new treaty was signed by the government and the Potawatomi among others, by which the government would purchase the Sugar Creek land in exchange for a reservation along the Kansas (Kaw) River [Chicoine 66-68; Garraghan 2.597-605]. By this time, the mission at Sugar Creek was going well, and the news of the coming move was dispiriting. Some of the Jesuits put a positive spin on it, arguing that the land was better in the new location, some ninety miles to the northwest. Lucile adopted this optimistic attitude when she wrote to Mother Barat on June 29, 1846, hoping for permission to move with the tribe. She reported not only that the land was better, but fishing as well, since they would be closer to a river. There would be no cost to the Society for two churches and two schools. The convent would be larger and better. The government was pleased, and it would be tragic to abandon the mission now.

While they were waiting for what would be a positive reply from Paris, a further letter of Lucile on August 19, 1846, describes a formal embassy on August 10, of four chiefs and other leaders, asking the religious to come with them. The same letter reports that they have eight boarders, children who live too far away to be day students like the larger number, who do all their own work, food preparation, etc., and care for the cows.

There had been an ongoing discussion since 1842 about extending the Society's mission to the Osage. A final abandonment of that proposal happened in spring or summer of 1847, for Lucile wrote to Mother Barat on July 12, 1847, of her regrets that the mission was not approved. They will probably move to "Kansas" in the fall, into a house that will be built during the summer. About this time, Lucile wrote of a dream she had, of a smiling young woman dressed in white. Lucile asked who she was, and her answer was Eugenie, said twice with something else that Lucile did not remember. Sometime later, they got word of the death of Eugenie de Gramont, RSCJ, in Paris on December 19, 1846. Lucile then had a similar dream of Elisabeth Galitzine, who had been instrumental in the establishment of the Indian mission and who had died in 1843. Lucile wrote that she took this as a sign that both loved the mission, since they came to see her.

The new place to which they moved, across the Kansas River, was from the first named St. Mary's Mission. It is possible that the earlier one at Sugar Creek also bore that name. Father Aelen in 1839 said that he would call the mission at Sugar Creek "Conceptio Beatae Mariae Virginis," Conception of the Blessed Virgin Mary. Yet it was popularly referred to as the Sugar Creek Catholic Mission, for example, in Father Verreydt's report to the government. September 30, 1843 [Garraghan 2. 196, 208].

Joseph Bertrand, who had been an important figure at Sugar Creek when they first arrived, had his house in the new location. The distance was about ninety miles, so the move was done over a period of days.[53] For the actual move, they assembled five

---

53 The move of the mission itself was more complicated. The Jesuits investigated several

*Waiguines* to hold their possessions. A little boy with a cart took the chickens, and someone else led the cows. The plan had been to move to "Kansas" in the fall of 1847, but that did not prove possible. Instead, it was nearly a year later, in September 1848, that they arrived there. The house journal recounts that most of the Indians arrived a week later, as well as the three Jesuits [*HJ*, 25-2].

A story is told of Lucile's courage and determination at this point: When some of the Indians arrived at the Kaw (Kansas) River after their long journey, they were discouraged and wanted to turn back to the nomadic life they had known. Ellen Craney,[54] who was not there, tells it simply: Lucile just leapt up and started clearing a space for a tent. Like all good stories, the details changed as it was retold. According to the account in the *Annual Letters,* Lucile took it upon herself to cross the river, jump from a wagon, and begin to cut down the tall prairie grass to make a path. The Indians were so astonished that they followed her example [*AL* 1876-1877, 2e, 275]. In that form it is problematic. According to the house journal [p. 25], she was already on the other side of the river when most of the Indians arrived, and there is no mention of this act on her part. Moreover, she would hardly have been able to cross the river on her own. The more plausible version is probably closer to Craney's. Nevertheless, the story reflects her courage and the high esteem in which everyone held her.

---

sites and a preliminary one was first chosen and occupied by November 1847, about seventeen miles south of the final one. Apparently the RSCJ did not plan to move until the final site was selected in June 1848 [Garraghan 2.600-605].

54 Ellen Craney, RSCJ, born in Rockford, Illinois, entered the Society in Chicago in 1871, made first vows in St. Louis in 1873, and spent her whole time of "aspirantship" (years before final profession) at St. Mary's. She was there until the closing, then returned to St. Louis, and died in Chicago in 1931.

# LIVING THE MISSION AT ST. MARY'S (1848-1868)

Lucile's letter to Mother Barat of November 13, 1848, says that they have been on the Kansas River since September 9. A two-room house was ready for them and a chapel had been built.[55] The government had given 2500 *piastres* (roughly equivalent to dollars) to build a school for forty-five students. They have fifty *arpents* (roughly equivalent to acres) and the same animals they had at Sugar Creek: two horses, five cows, and an undetermined number of chickens. Another letter reports that they will be paid $50 per year for each child, up to forty-six students, and the rest of the cost will be met by the parents.[56] In the school, they have eight boarders and twenty-six to thirty day students, but will not take more until spring, when they hope to get another sister and another English teacher.

At the time of the move, they had brought with them one sack of corn meal that lasted the whole time for all, with a *petit pain* each morning. They were surrounded by magnificent forest and plenty of *serpents sonnettes* (rattle snakes) that came into their cabins at night and stopped to look at a statue, gift of Mother Barat, of Mary crushing the serpent's head!

---

55 Lucile's report is as usual over-optimistic. The report of Father Maurice Gailland, SJ, described the houses as half finished, with no doors, windows, floors, or "any conveniences" (translation from Latin, Garraghan 2.605).
56 Philippine to Father Delacroix, February 10, 1850.

The allotment system was in practice here: instead of common use of land, according to the house journal, each Indian family got fifty *arpents* of land to cultivate, the same amount that the convent received. The government in 1849 was building for them a larger building, in which they hoped to be able to house fifty boarders and receive $50 each for their board. By the next May, they have fifty to sixty-nine Indian and half-breed students.[57] These details were reported by Philippine to Amelie Jouve[58] in Canada. It is remarkable how closely Philippine in St. Charles followed the life of the mission, to be able to report on it to others.

The community at St. Mary's felt their isolation from the rest of the vicariate. They do not know if they are in war or peace; they hear about the outside world once or twice a year. They rarely hear from other houses of the Society. Lucile asks permission to go sometimes to St. Louis or St. Charles, if someone has to go for health or some other reason, to presume permission if necessary because it would take too long to get a response. She reports in the same letter that they had had one visit from Elisabeth Galitzine at the beginning, and one from Reverend Mother Maria Cutts, superior at Grand Coteau and visitator of the Western houses, probably in 1847, but no other visitors from the Society.[59] They would not get another until 1856, and by that time, the results of the years of isolation in between would be telling. One connection they did have, however, she fails to

---

57 Letters of Philippine to Amelie Jouve at St-Vincent, Oct. 14, 1849; May 30, 1850.
58 Amelie Jouve, RSCJ (1799-1880), entered the Society in Paris in 1821 and made final profession in 1829. After the death of her saintly sister Euphrosine, in 1821, she adopted the name Aloysia, which Euphrosine had used. Amelie was sent to Canada in 1847, stopping on the way to visit her aunt Philippine in St. Charles. She became vicar of the western U.S. houses in 1855 and was superior at Grand Coteau from 1860 during the Civil War. She returned to France in 1879.
59 Reports on these two visits are not extant.

mention: there must have been regular correspondence with Philippine Duchesne in her last years in St. Charles. Philippine did not give up on her dream place. She reports in letters to Amelie Jouve in 1850 and Mother Barat in 1852 information that she had received in now non-extant letters, presumably from Lucile or someone else at the mission.

There are no surviving letters from Mother Barat to Lucile from April 1842 to February 1852, and again, nothing after September 1853, but there may be a reason for that. A biographer reports that she later destroyed her spiritual correspondence with Mother Barat [*Quelques contemporaines*, 123].

The community at St. Mary's was asked soon after the move to write an account of their life for the triennial reports in the *Annual Letters* of the Society. In spite of their move and the events surrounding it, Lucile wrote to Mother Cutts that there was nothing interesting to write about for the report. Nevertheless, the *Annual Letters* of 1848 or 1849 do contain a short description of their life. It compares their new location to the promised land because of its fertility and the abundance of fish, some of which are so large that they require two men to carry one (catfish, perhaps?), as well as an abundance of land animals: waterfowl, deer, turkeys, and ducks. Their two-room house is located in the middle of the village of 4,000, about half of whom are Christian, but the others willingly confide their children to the school. They are well supplied with corn and apples, but are very grateful for gifts from St. Michael of linens, sugar, coffee, and rice. There are three priests and five brothers among the Jesuits, along with one secular teacher.

# FIRST RETURN TO ST. LOUIS
# 1852

When a few years earlier Lucile asked in a letter to Mother Barat if she could presume permission to travel in case of some health difficulty, she may already have been aware that Louise Amiot was suffering from a lung problem. By 1852, she felt it necessary to take Louise to St. Louis for medical consultation. The account of the journey is given by Marie Monzert, RSCJ, who later briefly joined the St. Mary's community.[60]

The two set out in late May or early June for St. Louis by way of St. Joseph. Travel was by wagon over rough territory with very little habitation. One day on the road, the driver admitted he was lost, and they had to spend the night outdoors. While the driver, having imbibed too much whiskey, slept under the wagon, Lucile tried to cover Louise as best she could, fearful all night of possible attacks by wild animals.

They survived and reached St. Joseph, Missouri, on the Feast of the Sacred Heart, celebrated that year on June 18. There was not yet a convent of the Sacred Heart there, but they were kindly received by Father Scanlan, pastor of the only Catholic Church in the town, and given hospitality with an alumna from

---

60 Marie Rose Monzert, RSCJ, was born in Switzerland in 1828, entered the Society in St. Louis in 1847, and was professed in St. Louis in 1876. She met or became acquainted with Lucile at the stop in St. Joseph in 1852, later in St. Charles during Lucile's stay there, and seems to have been at St. Mary's for one year, 1868-1869, during Lucile's absence. She died in St. Charles in 1903.

St. Louis. They were not the first RSCJ to visit St. Joseph. Earlier in the year, Reverend Mother Cutts, vicar of the southern vicariate, and a companion had also received hospitality from Father Scanlan and one of at least three alumnae from Florissant and St. Charles. This time, the alumna from St. Charles probably knew Lucile from her years there. As with the visit of Mother Cutts earlier, the two religious were besieged with requests for a foundation in the town. They had received word that Mother Anna du Rousier[61] had arrived from France and was making her way around the Sacred Heart convents in North America, in order to give a report to the motherhouse in France. They thought she was already in St. Louis, and since that was the destination of Lucile and Louise, these two promised to convey the message. In fact, Mother du Rousier would not reach St. Louis for several months. Permission was given for a foundation in St. Joseph, which opened the next year.

The two travelers reached St. Louis after a journey of three weeks. The medical consultation was presumably done and may have helped. Louise would return to St. Mary's and survive another five years. The hope of finding Mother du Rousier already in St. Louis was not fulfilled, however. After waiting two weeks, they were obliged to return in the company of a Jesuit who could not wait any longer. During the time in St. Louis, however, Lucile was able to renew many old relationships from ten years earlier, to tell many stories about the mission, and to secure significant financial support from her friends. She must surely have gone to St. Charles to see her old friend Philippine, now in her final months; but Lucile had long gone at the time

---

61 Anna du Rousier, RSCJ, (1806-1880) served in Turin and Paris until she came as visitator to America in 1851. Instead of returning to France, however, she went from there as foundress to Chile, where she spent the rest of her life. She arrived in St. Louis in November 1852 in time to visit Philippine Duchesne just before her death.

of Anna du Rousier's arrival in St. Louis, her visit to the dying Philippine, and Philippine's death on November 18 of that year. The two travelers were back in St. Mary's by September 19, 1852, the day on which Louise made her final profession there. Though she had made first vows in 1837, her profession was delayed by the new regulations promulgated in the constitutional reforms of 1839.

# OFFICIAL VICARIATE VISITS (FROM 1856)

In 1851, the proposed new form of government for the Society, approved in 1839, had been set aside in favor of the appointment of superiors vicar for the various geographical regions. There had seemingly been no visits to St Mary's from any superior in the Society since 1847. An account of the foundation of St. Joseph in 1853 states that Mother Maria Cutts, then superior vicar of the southern United States houses, had visited St. Mary's in 1852, but there is no mention of such a visit in any document from St. Mary's. She may have intended it, but was prevented by flooding [Chicoine 93-94]. The house journal is missing from 1850 to 1856, but Lucile's letter to Mother Barat of February 26, 1853, speaks of Mother Cutts having sent a novice to the mission, but not of a visit by her superior. Likewise, Mother Gallwey, then superior in St. Louis,[62] was going to send a teacher, but the teacher died in the meantime. Again, no mention of a visit. The letter says that by February 1853, they were anticipating a visit by Mother du Rousier in her capacity as visitator from France, but there is no indication that she actually made it to St. Mary's. From St. Louis, she went to St. Joseph at the end of March for the beginning of that foundation. From there, it would have been the

---

62 Margaret Ann Gallwey (Galwey, Gallway) born in Ireland in 1805, entered the Society in 1836 at St. Michael and made her profession there in 1844. She was foundress in Chicago in 1858, then vicar of the West (1864-1869). She died in Chicago in 1873.

next step to St. Mary's. Again, there is no reference to such a visit in sources from St. Mary's. Rather, Mother du Rousier seems to have gone from there to Louisiana. Having finished her visit of all the houses, she returned to Buffalo, where she found the letter from Mother Barat asking her, rather than return to France, to go to Chile to make a foundation there. She and her two companions left New York for that long voyage in August 1853.

In the same letter of Lucile to Mother Barat, February 26, 1853, is a mysterious piece of information with regard to the possibility of local indigenous vocations to religious life. She reports that Mother Jacquet, superior at St. Charles, is

> happy with the two girls we sent them, and if we have more, to send them. They have taken the habit, which gave us great pleasure, also to the bishop and the father. We have another that I hope will respond to grace before long. We will let her desire mature. She is full of spirit, advanced in studies, and works toward her perfection.

Unfortunately, there are no further traces of these girls.

The 1854-1855 *Annual Letters* do not contain a current history of the mission, but an apology that nothing was received from St. Mary, and therefore two rather astounding letter fragments are included, the first, a letter from Bishop Miège[63] to an

---

63 Bishop John Baptist Miège, S.J. (1815-1884), consecrated bishop in St. Louis on March 25, 1851, was vicar apostolic to the "Indian Territory east of the Rocky Mountains," including most of what is now Kansas, Nebraska, Colorado, and Oklahoma, with about 5,000 Catholics. His first episcopal residence was St. Mary's, 1851-1855, then moved to Leavenworth, where, by the time of his resignation in 1874, there was a cathedral with 40,000 Catholics in the diocese. He retired to St. Louis, was later first president of Detroit College, and died in Woodstock, Maryland, in 1884.

unnamed superior of the Society.⁶⁴ It was not a way to win friends and supporters; in fact, given the way the letter patronizes the superior, it is surprising that it was published by the Society's motherhouse, usually very protective of those in authority. The bishop's letter accuses the anonymous superior of having an imagination that is *anti-Indienne*, falsely imagining that the religious there will lose the Sacred Heart spirit, by exaggerating the dangers, as if going back to the days of Christopher Columbus. He then details the spiritual resources available to them as well as the physical benefits. They have eighty boarding students (the end of the entry in the *AL* gives seventy-two), and if they are overworked, it is more her fault than his. He warns that Lucile and Mary Ann O'Connor will soon be *hors de combat*, and who will replace them?

Lucile's letter follows immediately, addressed to Mother Jouve by name, beginning with *Nous voulons aussi*.... not a way to begin a point but to continue it, though the tone of her letter is conciliatory and respectful. She warns that when Mother Jouve comes, she will find that they are not all saints. They live in an episcopal city, on the military route to California, so no one should be afraid to join them in this "lost" land.⁶⁵ She too stresses the abundance of spiritual resources available to them.

By the mid-1850s, much had changed on the Potawatomi mission, as Lucile describes in her letter. Was the bishop exaggerating, and did Amelie Jouve remember too clearly her aunt's

---

64 Callan, 297, gives a translation of the text and assumes the recipient is Margaret Gallwey, then superior in St. Louis (also Chicoine 92-94), but her source is the *AL* itself, which does not name the recipient. More likely, it was addressed to Aloysia Jouve, who had just been named vice-vicar for the southern houses in the United States, and was the named recipient of Lucile's letter that follows. The correspondence is published instead of a report in order "to make this interesting mission known and loved."
65 *AL* 1854-1855, X. 29-30. It was on or very near the Oregon Trail that began in Independence, Missouri, and was at its height in the early 1850s.

descriptions of the privations of the early years at Sugar Creek and assume that it was still the same at St. Mary's? They were soon to find out. In June of 1856, Mother Amelie (Aloysia) Jouve came for what was finally an official visit of a superior. One wonders with what attitude she arrived, after a superior, perhaps herself, was dressed down the year before by the bishop in the *Annual Letters* for the whole Society to read.

Amelie Jouve, RSCJ (1799-1880)

The house journal, silent since a short entry for 1850, resumes with a summary dated 1856 [*HJ* 26]. It states clearly that the house had not had a visit from a vicar since the first year with Mother Galitzine. Now, Mother Jouve came, accompanied by Hyacinthe Cutts (sister of former vicar Mother Maria Cutts, who had died in 1854), and Sisters Bridget O'Neil[66] and Elizabeth Schrader,[67] who were to join the community. According to Elizabeth's account, they came by riverboat as far as Leavenworth, where they received hospitality from Bishop Miège, who had moved his residence there from St. Mary's in 1855. He provided a carriage to take them the two days to St. Mary's. When they arrived in late June 1856, neither she nor Mother Jouve was impressed. Elizabeth Schrader compared the poor little house to the beauty of Grand Coteau, from which she had come. Amelie Jouve, in her report to Mother Barat, written from St. Mary's on July 4, mailed later from St. Louis, described a miserable assembly of about a hundred small cabins scattered in the woods, a poor place with an overcrowded eighty boarders, for each of whom the government each year gave $375. She admits that the food is better than in many houses, but contrasts the cleanliness of the fathers' house with the disorder of the religious. They must build a new house. The Jesuit superior (Father Duerinck, S.J.) is their *econome*; Lucile is his "humble servant," who never asks for a report and never gets one.

---

66 Bridget O'Neil, RSCJ, born in Ireland in 1818, emigrated at the age of 15, and entered in St. Charles in 1841. Her profession date was set in 1856 with her destination set for St. Mary's, but there was an urgent reason to leave before the ceremony could take place, so her profession was made in the cathedral of Bishop Miège in Leavenworth, Kansas, on June 24. She then spent twenty-three years at St. Mary's, there until the end. She died the next year, 1880, in St. Louis.

67 Elizabeth Schrader (Shrader, Schroeder) was born in Germany in 1829, immigrated to the United States and entered the Society in Grand Coteau in 1852, where she made her first vows in 1855. Her final profession was made at St. Mary's in 1862. She remained there until its closure in 1879, then went to Chicago, where she died in 1903.

An outside witness to life at the mission, remembered many years later, may help to illustrate what life was like there, and why Lucile was happy to have the Jesuits handle the money. Much later, in 1894, Father Francis Stuntebeck, SJ, who replaced Fr. Duerinck after the latter's death in 1857, remembered some aspects of life at the mission, including how difficult it was to get the government subsidy and why the finances of both groups were combined:

> As you will see, they got $50 per year for boarding + clothing the Indian girls + $12 per year for Day scholars. Fr. Verreydt made out a similar report for the boys, giving each one's name + the length of time that he had been at school. To this he added the report for the girls: it was then transmitted to the Indian agent of the Reservation, who had to state that the record was all right, then the report in duplicate was sent to St Louis, to F. DeSmet, or whoever had his place in his absence: thence it was sent to the Indian Comissionary at Washington, who signed it + sent it to the Interior Department, here again it had to be signed + transmitted to the Treasurer of the U.S. who finally made out a voucher for the amount + sent it back to St Louis. This was then collected + the Potawatomie Mission credited by the amount.
>
> The Superior of the Mission came to St Louis once a year (or else sent his requisition) to lay in a stock of Groceries and Dry Goods for both communities, + each got a share: the sisters made the clothes for

the girls, the brother for the boys. In other respects the two communities were almost one. The sisters milked the cows + made the butter for both. In the spring when the ground was soft, a brother frequently accompanied the sisters to the cow yard to fish out with a pitchfork, their shoes which stuck in the mud, frequently ankle deep. For the rest of course the communities were separate. So you see that the sisters had very little use for Book-Keeping. If any money was over the expenses, it was laid out for the benefit of each community as occasion might require. [autograph GASSH]

Aloysia Jouve's letter reporting to Mother Barat skims the top of her concerns, more deeply revealed in the memorial that she wrote on July 8 and left at St. Mary's, the customary notes of commendations and recommendations that a visiting superior traditionally left behind. She begins with regret that the mission has been so long without the visit of a vicar and helpful advice about advancing in virtue. The only way to maintain the union and spirit of the Society, she asserts, is by strict adherence to the rules, a generally accepted norm in the religious life of the day, enshrined in fact in the *Constitutions* (Summary XXVI). As would become clear, the years of separation and lack of communication with others in the Society, along with the poverty and daily hardships, meant that quite naturally, a series of differences of observance had arisen at St. Mary's. She commends them for their devotion to the Indians and their excellence as teachers. But, she adds, they are to be not only teachers but also religious. Among the small infractions she lists, there should be only two objects of piety (statues, pictures, etc.) in a room and no pictures on the walls. Cleanliness is neglected, but each religious should have only two habits that can be worn in every season. (She is there in July!) The school enrollment is too big; there should be no more than seventy boarders, and a new building is needed for the community. The superior will see her daughters more often for spiritual direction, and, in keeping with the sacramental discipline of the times, she should not give permission to receive Holy Communion on Saturday, except to those practicing virtue or having repaired their faults.

More substantive are the comments with regard to the distinctions that had developed in other larger houses of the Society between the choir and coadjutrix religious, amounting to a class system. In this small and crowded house, with only four of each rank, it is difficult to imagine how they could have maintained traditional differences, even if they had wanted to, which, it seems, Lucile did not. So a precise set of instructions with regard to conformity to usages and rules follows. The sisters must wear a habit of heavier material and all the same. Habits cannot be passed from choir to coadjutrix, and their places in the chapel must distinguish them by rank.

Counting the two who arrived with Mother Jouve, there would now be five choir religious: Lucile, Mary Ann O'Connor, Julia Deegan, Bridget O'Neil, and Elizabeth Schrader; also four coadjutrix sisters: Mary Layton, Louise Amiot, Bridget Barnwell, and Margaret Mahony (Mahuny).[68]

Mother Jouve came and went. Her concluding memo is dated July 8. When Lucile writes to Mother Cahier at the motherhouse in Paris on December 12, 1856, she speaks of the joy brought by the visit of Reverend Mother Vicar, with no mention of her complaints. She reports that nothing is lacking for their tempo-

---

68  For more detail on the report of the visit, see Chicoine 94-100.

ral needs, and she leaves it to Reverend Mother Vicar to tell them more. Great progress is being made, she reports, in teaching the Indians to cultivate the ground and to raise pigs for food.

All are well except Louise Amiot, who has spent six weeks in her room, very ill with disease of the chest; she will not recover (*de la poitrine* normally meant tuberculosis). In spite of the trip to St. Louis for medical consultation five years earlier, she would live only a few more months, dying on February 26, 1857, at the age of thirty-nine, the first of the original mission band, other than Philippine, to die.

One thing at least was done in response to Mother Jouve's critique: the number of boarders was reduced to seventy, but not for long. By the report in the *Annual Letters* of 1862, the number was back to eighty, with only one day student, a Protestant. Meanwhile, however, the *Annual Letters* account of early 1858 tells of the visit of Mother Jouve in June-July 1856, the death of Louise Amiot in February 1857, and that of John Duerinck, S.J., the resident Jesuit superior who had been the community's agent and financial manager. His death occurred under tragic and unclear circumstances, by drowning in the Missouri River while traveling, sometime between November 24 and December 14, 1857 [Garraghan 2.674-75]. This loss was compensated by several visits from Pierre DeSmet, SJ, the famous missionary, including one long visit on his way back from the *lac salé* (Salt Lake) where he had taken part in an expedition "against the Mormons."

The *Annual Letters* of 1862 report on the success of training Indian girls to be good Christian mothers of families. At one visit of Bishop Miège, he gave the sacrament of Confirmation to thirty-two children who had made their First Communion. Tragically, four children died while at the school in 1861. In one case, the grandmother came to take the sick child home, but she did not want to leave, since she had not yet made her First Communion; she died there two days later. At another episcopal visit, they celebrated the final profession of Elizabeth Schrader on May 5, 1862.

A few months later, the community lost Mary Ann O'Connor, whose peaceful death occurred on December 8, 1863. She and Lucile had been together in St. Charles and then in Kansas for thirty-five years. At this point, Lucile was the only remaining one of the four pioneers who had come to Sugar Creek in 1841.[69]

On May 29, 1866, the foundation at St. Mary's received another official visit from the superior vicar, this time Reverend Mother Margaret Gallwey, accompanied by Mother Regis Hamilton, at this point assistant superior in Chicago and one of the vicariate consultors. The community account in the *Annual Letters* of 1866 reports their joy at the visit. "Everyone hurried to receive her good advice and try to put it into practice." A somewhat different tone was invoked in the opening remarks of Mother Gallwey's note of her visit:

> The different abuses specified by Rev. Mother Jouve during her visit in 1856, have not been attended to, they still exist, it is useless for Supr. Vicar's [sic] to make their visits if the Local Superiors do not have their directions carried out.

---

69 Born probably in 1785 in Ireland, Mary Ann O'Connor made her first vows in 1825 in Florissant, accompanied Philippine Duchesne to the foundation of City House in 1827, then was one of the refounders of St. Charles with Lucile in 1828, where she was professed the next year.

Margaret Gallwey, RSCJ (1805-1873)

Apparently Mother Jouve's effort ten years earlier to make this little prairie band conform to more regimented customs observed in larger houses of the Society was of no avail. They lived their life as they had to in order to accomplish their goals. As with the earlier visit by Amelie Jouve, there were again many small regulations that were to be carried out. Several make us wonder.

"All the Sisters are to wear sleeves."

"No Sister can go out of the gate for the Cows."

Most surprising to the contemporary reader, perhaps, is that in keeping with the sacramental discipline of the day, reception of Holy Communion was seen as a reward for the worthy. Anyone who failed in charity or spoke unnecessarily during times of silence was to forego Communion until the fault was repaired by acknowledgement to the superior.

They were now eleven in the community, five choir religious and six coadjutrix sisters, and ninety-six students. A general portrait of Lucile in these years by those who remembered her was of someone who was always easy on others and hard on herself. She reveled in the physical hardship of their living situation. She seemed able to do anything and took on the worst jobs for herself. She was often roused during the night by Indians coming to ask for prayer or help of some kind. A saying of uncertain origin described Lucile and her relationship to the Indians in those years: "They made use of this mother as one uses water, without thinking of it, because they were sure of always finding her ready and life-giving."[70]

When their farm animals were dying of hunger, she freed and sent off the last cow so she would not see it die. They were all surprised the next year to see it return, quite well, with a calf. It was said that a bishop (probably Bishop Miège, who lived at St. Mary's 1851-1855, his first years in office) suggested that she sing when she was suffering too much. When others heard her singing, they knew what it meant. [*Quelque contemporaines*, 122].

---

70 Quoted as someone else's saying by Thompson, 110.

By the 1860s, the change to white presence in the two schools was being felt. Yet one Irish American boy found himself the only one in his class who was not Indian. James J. Conway, SJ, entered the Jesuit school in 1863, and found his classmates very rough. When he tired of them, he used to go over to the convent, sit down by Mother Mathevon, put his head on her shoulder and cry. As his deceased mother would have done, she comforted him until he was able to go back. He later said that without her, he would not have been able to remain at St. Mary's [Craney].

# YEARS IN EXILE FROM ST. MARY'S (1868-1871)

Things were changing, however, from the happy little group that had found its own way of working together in extreme poverty. Mother Gallwey returned in November 1868. By this time, Lucile was seventy-five years old, had been superior for twenty-eight years, and was not well. She suffered now from a "humiliating and incurable" medical condition [*HJ*, 28]. It was the judgment of the superior vicar that she must leave this difficult mission for somewhere less rigorous. Judging from Mother Gallwey's report after her 1866 visit, it was also certainly clear that in her judgment Lucile was less than adequate as a superior. The occasion of her poor health was also a way to relieve her of that burden. When Mother Gallwey left on November 19, Lucile left with her under obedience, a painful separation for all, but especially for Lucile. Ellen Milmoe, who had been at St. Mary's since 1866, became superior at the mission from 1869 to 1871.[71] At that time, Mary Ann Armstrong, RSCJ, came from St. Louis to be superior for the rest of Lucile's time there, until 1877.[72]

---

71 Ellen Milmoe, RSCJ, was born in Ireland in 1827, emigrated with her family in 1845, entered in St. Louis in 1854, and made final profession in Chicago in 1864. After a short time in St. Mary's and life in several other houses, she died in St. Louis in 1891.
72 Mary Ann Armstrong, RSCJ, born in Ireland in 1827, came to the U.S. at age fifteen, entered the Society in St. Louis in 1856, was professed in Chicago in 1863, and died in St. Louis in 1885.

Other things were changing at St. Mary's as well. The railroad had arrived nearby by 1866, facilitating much more population movement. The broken promises of the government to the Potawatomi that this would be their land forever were meaningless. More and more white settlers were moving in, buying land from the Indians, and entering into many integrated marriages. The Potawatomi were retreating from the area, migrating to the south, and the government subsidies were disappearing. If the school was to remain open, it had to adjust to this new population who wanted a different kind of education for their children. Permission had to be obtained from superiors to take them into the boarding school, paid by the parents, not the government. By 1870, it was no longer seen as a school to educate Indians, and the government stopped paying the Jesuits and therefore the RSCJ. The 1870 census lists fifteen religious, of whom nine were born in Ireland, seven "teachers" (choir religious) and eight "domestic servants" (coadjutrix sisters).

On May 25, 1869, at a meeting at the Leavenworth residence of Bishop Miège, an agreement was drawn up with the Jesuits, ceding specific pieces of property to the RSCJ so that they could build a new building. Representatives of the Society were Reverend Mother Gallwey, vicar of the West, and Reverend Mother Mary Ann Aloysia Hardey, Vicar of the East, the latter probably because of her renowned financial expertise. According to the agreement, the Jesuits would cede to the Society fifty to sixty acres that included the current residence and room for a large building with playgrounds, garden, orchard, and pasture, plus ten milk cows—more if needed—and some other livestock, $10,000 cash, and provisions for a year and a half if needed.[73] Until this point, property, resources, and finances had been

---

73 Original copy USCA; summary Garraghan 3.56.

shared under the administration of the Jesuits. Now, the Society would manage its finances independently.

Though not recorded in the house journal, the agreement was preceded by a visit of Mothers Gallwey and Hardey. A long and descriptive account of their visit and the mission in 1869 was written by Mother Hardey's secretary, Margaret Hoey,[74] to the community at Kenwood. Among other things, she cited that

> The convent, a frame building in the rear of the Jesuit College, might be taken for one of the out-houses. There is no plastering in any part of the house, the ceilings and walls are of whitewashed muslin. In the parlor and next best room the muslin is covered with colored paper, and the floor is of rough planks.... Near the convent are two little huts, I cannot give them any other name. In one we found the kitchen and the pupils' refectory....In the second hut was the refectory of the community. The room was rather miserable looking, but we had white stoneware instead of tin (as for the pupils), and everything looked neat and clean The next apartment was the community dormitory, containing four beds. In the middle of the room is a little altar, on which is a statue of the Blessed Virgin, resembling a squaw, and pasted on the wall are four angels in gilt paper and cut in most fantastic shapes. We named it the 'Chapel of the Angels.'[75]

---

[74] Margaret Hoey, RSCJ (1839-1917), born of Irish parents in New York, entered the Society at Manhattanville in 1839 and made her profession at Kenwood in 1867. She was treasurer there, then personal secretary to Reverend Mother Hardey in 1870, including part of Mother Hardey's time as assistant general in Paris. She was later superior in several places and died at Eden Hall in Philadelphia.

[75] Original letter not extant, fuller quotes in Garvey, 292-294.

During the visit, one of the visitors asked one of the Sisters how many of the fifty cows and 25 calves the Fathers owned. Her answer was that both groups owned them all. This was the beloved poor and simple house that Lucile had loved and recently had to leave. The new agreement after her departure paved the way for the school to form a legal corporation as Sacred Heart Academy in December 1869, with assets judged to be $30,000. They were now a regular boarding school. In the legal document of erection of the corporation, the first members of the board of trustees were: Margaret Milmoe, Bridget O'Neil, Mary T. Dowdall,[76] Elizabeth Schrader, and Mary Leyton.[77] The new four-story building, the "skyscraper of the prairie," was going up, and they moved into it in September 1871 [*HJ*, 27]. Finally, then they were able to keep the Eucharist in their own house. For all the previous years, they had trudged in snow or mud in the morning to Mass in the Jesuit chapel. Bishop Miège, who had spent his first years as bishop there (1851-1855), said that he had never suffered so much from the cold as in that church [*AL* 1877, p. 277].

At this point, the whole previous plan of education had changed. Instead of the 70+ Indian boarders of earlier days, there were now 26 boarders, 23 day students, and 13 in the parish school, which they also staffed. Two of the boarding students from those years entered the Society.[78]

---

76 Mary Teresa Dowdall, RSCJ, born in Ireland in 1838, emigrated to America, entered the Society at Grand Coteau in 1855, and was professed in Chicago in 1866. She came to St. Mary's in 1869 and was there until the end. She then returned to Chicago, from where she later went to Timaru, New Zealand, and died there in 1887.
77 Her name is usually spelled Layton, but on this documentit it is corrected to Leyton.
78 Katherine Ann Caplice, RSCJ (1859-1911) and Johanna Hanrahan, RSCJ (1857-1944); cf. Chicoine 119.

All of this was happening while Lucile was away. She had returned to St. Charles, where she had previously lived for thirteen years, from 1828 to departure for Kansas in 1841. She had hoped to be able to return quickly to St. Mary's, but a letter from Mother Josephine Goetz, superior general, in March 1869 dashed those hopes. Lucile took it with faith, and began to enter into life in St. Charles. The St. Mary's community by this time had thirteen members, much larger than in early days, but at St. Charles there were twenty-three, an even larger community. For the years that she would spend there, she was listed in the Society Catalog simply as a member of the community council. Nevertheless, she taught First Communion preparation for the francophone children of the parish. The pastor also gave her the task of instructing little poor boys, first in the sacristy of the church, then in the school building. Many of her former students from years ago were still near. They were overjoyed to hear of her return, and often came to visit her [*AL* 1876-1877].

During Lucile's absence from St. Mary's, there was another vicariate visit in October 1869, this time by Reverend Mother Rose Gauthreaux.[79] At this time, there were five choir religious and eight sisters. Among a number of small observations is once again the necessity of maintaining the distinction between the two orders: "The choir religious are too free with the sisters." Reverend Mother Gauthreaux was back in April 1870, with a few more observations, among them: "The Indian children's dresses are made too wide and too short in the waist, and too long in the skirt." This suggests a different uniform for the Indian students and white students.

---

79 Mary Rose Gauthreaux, RSCJ, born in New Orleans in 1825, raised as an orphan at St. Michael, entered there in 1840 and was professed at Eden Hall in 1855. She was vicar of the West 1869-1872, and died in Chicago in 1872.

*Lucile Mathevon, RSCJ (1793-1876)*

Rose Gauthreaux, RSCJ (1825-1872)

# RETURN AND FINAL YEARS AT ST. MARY'S (1871-1876)

Lucile, however, was languishing. Away from her beloved mission and the Indians, she could not really be happy. On the other end, the remaining Potawatomi were unhappy without her, too. Their insistence and that of many others that she come back was finally acknowledged when it went as far as the motherhouse in Paris, and Reverend Mother Gauthreaux in St. Louis acceded to their wishes, permitting Lucile to return to her beloved St. Mary's in 1871.

She arrived by train, now conveniently passing nearby, on November 14, 1871. Her return was a triumph. A large group of people, Indians and others, were waiting for her at the station. She was accompanied by Reverend Mother Gauthreaux, now vicar, Mother Tardiu,[80] and Sr. Palmer.[81] Knowing St. Mary's to be the poorest house in the vicariate, now with a new chapel, they brought gifts of sacristy items [*HJ*, 30]. One gentleman simply picked up Lucile and carried her to the waiting carriage and to her home. For several weeks, she was inundated with Indian friends who came to see her. A table was set out for them, with cake, apples, and candy. The joy of everyone at her return

---

80 Catherine de Tardiu, RSCJ, was born 1810 in France, came to America with E. Galitzine in 1843, and returned 1851-1875. She is credited with compiling the journal of St. Mary's to 1872. She died in Toulouse in 1889.
81 Probably Mary Palmer, born in Ireland 1840, entered the Society in Chicago in 1862, and died there in 1932.

was touching. Many things were different, however. There were many more whites coming to settle in the area and the town. The religious no longer lived in a poor log cabin, but in a new brick building of several stories. She lamented the fact that muddy shoes were not allowed in the hall, that furniture had to be handled gently, etc. [Craney]. Most of the students were now the children of white farmers. She was overheard to say: "This is no longer my dear mission of long ago!" [*AL* 1876-1877]

The new building put their finances in a precarious position in January 1872 that brought Mother Gauthreaux back to work on it for three days. They had been paying off the debt to a Mr. McGonigle by one or two hundred *piastres* (nearly equivalent to dollars) per month. Suddenly he insisted, because of a wider financial crisis caused by the great Chicago fire, that he must have $8,000 at once. There was no way to borrow; the banks were overwhelmed. The religious appealed to the motherhouse in Paris; they agreed to help, but it would take until April 1 to assemble the funds. With great prayer by all, Mr. McGonigle was persuaded to wait until April 1, but on that date, they still had only $1,000. At that point, an Indian woman, hearing of their disstress, loaned them 1,000 *piastres*, interest free. The bank then granted three more grace days, until April 3. On April 3, $6150 arrived from the mother general. The uneven sum indicated that she scraped together everything she could. Then Reverend Mother Aloysia Hardey sent $10,000 from the house in Havana, loaned at 8%. At that, their debts were paid, with some left over.

The situation, along with several other factors, prompted another official visit, this time by Reverend Mother Hardey in April 1872. Reverend Mother Gauthreaux had died on March 26. Mother Hardey had been appointed assistant general in

The "Skyscraper of the Prairie" (1870)
Photo: Maureen Chicoine, RSCJ

late 1871, which necessitated her making visits to all the houses before moving to Paris. She and her unnamed traveling companion(s), probably her secretary Mother Hoey, set out from St. Joseph by coach at seven in the evening. In the middle of the night, they had to change carriages at an unknown destination, and at three o'clock in the morning, the coachman announced that they had arrived at St. Mary's. The telegram they had sent announcing their arrival had not come through, and there was no one there to meet them. They sat for a while, but it was soon too cold to stay in one place, so they began walking, until they saw a light in a house, where they were well received and eventually brought to their destination [*AL* 1872-1873].

The memorial of the visit left by Reverend Mother Hardey on April 18 exhorts them to buy stoves to heat the buildings, but not otherwise to incur more expenses until the debts are paid off, $6150 in two years to the motherhouse, the other to Havana semi-annually via the treasurer of the Manhattanville foundation. By October 1873, the total debt was $26,650, but the interest on the Havana debt had been lowered by Mother Hardey. By June 12, 1875, the debt had been reduced to $4,400 [*HJ*, 31-33]. Lucile was not superior in these years, but as a member of the community, she had to live through the anxiety of a situation so different from the simple dependent poverty she had known in the earlier years.

Through the years, from the first visit of Amelie Jouve in 1866, the question of the relationships among the choir religious and coadjutrix sisters had been a problem. While in the larger houses elsewhere in the Society, the distinction was falling into recognized lines, it simply was not possible in what had been a small informal group, and several times, a superior coming from outside did not understand that these differences were not only not helpful but not feasible here. After Lucile's departure in 1868, other superiors who followed seem to have made greater efforts to carry out this mandate, perhaps with too much zeal. Mother Hardey now found the differences overdone, to the extent of a failure in charity. She admonished the choir religious to show great kindness to the sisters

> who have hitherto been treated rather harshly and in a manner so contrary to the spirit of the Society. No distinction should be made in the food served to the Sisters in the Refectory, nor should the cast off clothing of the Choir religious be distributed to them.

Apparently the problem did not go away. When Reverend Mother Tucker, then vicar, made her visit in 1875, she could still write in her memorial on June 12 that there was "a want of love and cordiality" between choir and sisters. She reflected that "having been formerly on an equal footing with the Choir religious has in some measure contributed to the existing feelings, but charity demands that a remedy be applied," which included "never speaking to them with a tone of authority—never reprehending them, especially before the pupils." It must have been difficult for Lucile, who had so nourished community spirit during her years of leadership, to experience now this ongoing discrepancy.

Other events marked their life. One was the death of Julia Deegan, RSCJ, on December 20, 1872.[82] She died of an unspec-

---

82  Born in Ireland in 1825, she was one of the thousands of Irish immigrants to America. She entered the Society in St. Louis in 1849, and already as a novice was sent to St. Mary's, where she made her first vows in 1851 and final profession in 1860.

ified long illness at the age of forty-seven. She was the first deceased RSCJ to be buried in the new convent cemetery, where she joined the bodies of Louise Amiot and Mary Ann O'Connor, transferred there in 1869 from the mission chapel cemetery.[83] In early 1973, a wave of smallpox was all around the mission, but they were mercifully spared.

Prayerbook used by Lucile [USCA]

During these last five years until her death, Lucile was listed in the Society Catalog as community counsellor and *infirme*. Every morning, she was in the chapel for Mass and Holy Communion. After breakfast, she returned for several hours, then visited Mary

---

83 Chicoine, 78-79.

Layton, her longtime companion, who was paralyzed that last fourteen months of her life. The later part of the day would find Lucile again in prayer [*AL* 1876-1877]. The description is poignantly reminiscent of the account of Philippine's days there in 1841-1842. Like Philippine, Lucile's role in the mission was now prayer.

Ellen Craney remembered Lucile in her old age as not striking:

> rather bent, but firm on her feet, complexion sallow, eyes large and bulging, the whites glazed; teeth remarkable, large, strong, she never had a toothache! Kind and gentle, she welcomed us with a sweet smile. She had been a great laugher in early days—a fact that helped much to carry her through pioneer difficulties and made her wonderfully forbearing.

By Christmas 1875, Lucile was growing weaker and longing to be "taken to Paradise" by the infant Jesus, but wrote to someone that her task on earth was not yet finished. On March 10, 1876, she was taken to the infirmary with a light lung congestion that the doctor assured was nothing serious. She declined the offer of one of the community to keep watch. During the middle hours of the night, she was found unconscious, and soon after sacramental anointing, she breathed her last, in the early hours of March 11, 1876.

Word spread quickly of her death. The next day, her body was brought to the chapel, where crowds of Indians and whites came to see her and touch their rosaries and medals to her mortal remains.

The day she was buried the Indians, who had gathered from all the country around, hovered near her grave till nightfall, moaning, crying gently, the saddest looking people I ever saw. No wonder, what had she not done for them! She was the first white woman who put foot in what is now St. Mary's. [Craney]

Lucile and Mary Layton had been together since 1845, except for the few years that Lucile was in St. Charles. Mary, too, longed to finish her time on earth. She had been completely paralyzed during that last fourteen months, and Lucile promised that if she died first, she would come for her. Just 21 days later, she kept her promise. Mary died on March 30, 1876.

Both were buried in the convent cemetery on the northwest side of the property, alongside those who had been their companions in life. The Jesuit College continued on the site for many years.[84] In 1909, a gymnasium was built in the area, necessitating the move of the remains from the original cemetery to the common Catholic Cemetery of the town of St Marys. A letter of Fr. A.J. Reid, SJ, to Reverend Mother Vicar Angela McCabe, RSCJ, on November 12, 1950, quotes Fr. Augustine Wand, SJ, "our historian and archivist at St. Mary's":

> Fr. Wand told me to tell you that someone of your Society should write a life of Mother Lucille Mathevon. He believes that she was both a very remarkable and a very holy woman. He tells me too that when the remains of these early Missionaries

---

[84] For the subsequent history of the property, see Chicoine, *Grave on the Prairie*, pp. 142-144.

were being transferred to their present resting place, those of Mother Mathevon were inclosed [*sic*] in a special box, so that they might be more easily recognized as being hers [USCA].

All were then interred in the common grave that stands today in the Catholic cemetery.

Gravemarker of the Religious of the Sacred Heart,
Mt. Calvary Cemetery, St. Marys, Kansas.
Photo: Maureen Chicoine, RSCJ

# CONCLUSION

No account of the mission-schools at St. Mary's is adequate which does not leave the reader with an impression of the important share of the Religious of the Sacred Heart in making them a success. In their hands ever since the days of Mother Duchesne at Sugar Creek was the education of the Potawatomi girls; that they acquitted themselves with distinction of this phase of the missionary program of St. Mary's is a fact written large in the story of the mission.... The names of scarcely any of their number found their way into contemporary records. It was enough for them that they gave themselves unreservedly to the task in hand, that they spared neither time nor energy nor available means of whatsoever kind.... [Garraghan 3.54].

The name of Lucile Mathevon is writ large across the story of the mission, unacknowledged in much of the public story telling for many years in the shadow of Philippine Duchesne, though recognized by those who knew her and knew the history.

Today we may judge differently about the efforts of Lucile and her companions to change Native Americans with traditional beliefs and nomadic way of life into agriculturalist Christians, indigenous girls into "good Christian mothers of families." Even so, we must acknowledge their indomitable courage and sincere belief that they were giving them not less but more, not destroying but providing a wider and fuller life, and enabling necessary skills to face the inevitable changes that were happening all around them. The ability of women like Lucile Mathevon to step into the unknown and create a meaningful life lived for others there continues to convey its challenge to our world.

# EPILOGUE

It had been long apparent that St. Mary's was no longer able to fulfill its original purpose, the dream of Philippine and Lucile, and the numbers of students were dwindling. In its last year, there were sixteen students, not one with any Indian blood. On February 10, 1879, the Jesuit school, ten-year-old St. Mary's College, burnt to the ground. The RSCJ offered their spacious brick building, not fully occupied, to the Jesuits. This was the occasion to act, and Reverend Mother Vicar Susannah Boudreau soon made the necessary decision to close the foundation. She said it was the hardest thing she had ever had to do. By this time, the Potawatomi in the area were dwindling and moving on, many to a new reservation in Oklahoma [Garraghan 3.57-65; Chicoine 105-120].

Mother Boudreau was rewarded, however, by being asked by the motherhouse the next year to assemble from St. Louis the band of missionaries who would go to make a foundation in Timaru, New Zealand. While none of the final group from St. Mary's was part of that first band, it was the freeing of the twenty-four religious who were there for other work that enabled the new mission in Oceania. By God's mystery, Susannah Boudreau would die there within a month of her arrival, but Lucile's mission was carried on in a new part of the world.

# APPENDICES

### 1. Journal of the Crossing, 1821-1822
### by Lucile Mathevon, RSCJ

*The two missionaries, Lucile Mathevon and Anna Murphy, RSCJ, journeyed first to Bordeaux, staying with the religious there; then to Pauillac where they were to board ship. As the elder, Lucile wrote their farewell letter to the community in Bordeaux.*[85]

Lucile Mathevon to Josephine Bigeu, Bordeaux

Bordeaux, Pauillac
December 6, 1821

For Reverend Mother Bigeu

Dear Reverend Mother,

    I hasten to give you news of us, so you will not worry about us and at the same time to satisfy myself because I have great satisfaction in speaking to you again of France. I did not believe in holding on to this dear country, and when I thought of leaving it, I felt great sorrow. But I quickly sacrificed it for our good Master, and I no longer have any sorrow, I am in the joy of my soul. I have no fear, neither of rivers nor of the sea; I have been very content all the time I have been here.

---

85 French autograph. GASSH CVII 2. Transcription Paisant, L. 116, pp. 437-38. Josephine Bigeu was superior of the new community there and Lucile's former mistress of novices. A post-script added to the first page: "The pastor asks me to offer his respects to Mother Lalanne."

We have very good passengers, all very respectable; there are three women who all have children of eleven, five and two years old; there is an Irish gentleman who knows the family of Sister Xavier very well; he is very kind to us. Sister Xavier has given him news of his family, as he has not had news of them for a long time. All the merchandise on this ship is his, so that he is like the master and treats us accordingly. The sick woman who came with us manages her fatigue with great courage.

We have been well received by the pastor of Pauillac; nothing has been lacking to us: a three-course meal, coffee, rum, in sum, all sorts of kindnesses. He has an Irish vicar; Sister Xavier is very happy with him. She was charmed to find a compatriot. She is only troubled about leaving too early.

We embark today, December 6$^{th}$ at four in the evening. Please, dear mother, give this news to Mother Barat and to the house at Grenoble. We ask in a special way for the prayers of all the Society. On our side, we will not forget this dear Society, and particularly the house of Bordeaux. Give my regards to Father Barat as well as to all our Fathers. Please give Mother Lalanne all the gratitude we owe her for so much goodness, and the same to Mrs. Fournier and to Mrs. Dubourg.[86] My love to all my dear sisters.

It is in union with the Divine Hearts that I ask you to accept the assurance of my respect and the tender attachment of your unworthy daughter,

Lucile Mathevon

---

86 Victoire Fournier, sister of Bishop Louis William Dubourg, and her sister-in-law, wife of the bishop's brother.

Journal of the voyage, by Lucile Mathevon[87]

Dear Reverend Mother,

It is only on the eighth day that I can write to you; it has been impossible to do so earlier. But fearing to omit any circumstances of our dear voyage, I give them with great difficulty as the rolling of the ship is so strong that at each moment I roll to the side of my cabin. I am sufficiently recovered finally to tell you all that we are doing and the good company that we have had the good fortune to encounter.

We see well that the Lord watches over us and that we are accompanied by the prayers of our good mothers and sisters. It is a blessing of God over us that these gentlemen do not cease to admire, and they say that we are children of Providence. We have, however, had much to suffer from contrary winds for nineteen days, but the sea has always been in our favor. Here is a first point of their admiration, and they say: "It is astonishing that with a wind so strong and so contrary, all on board have been happy!" It is only I who have experienced great fear. I spent the nights in prayer, and sometimes I woke Sister Xavier, who told me to be still, that she never sleeps better than when the sea is agitated. I admire her tranquility.

Finally, I must add a word about our companions, of whom we are the spoiled children: eight gentlemen, of whom six are from New Orleans and two from Philadelphia,[88] and three ladies from New Orleans. They are very respectful and do not permit any bad language in our company. They are very reserved and show us great respect. They wanted us to be placed at table next

---

87 French copy GASSH A II 2 j, Box 3: *Lettres intéressantes,* cahier 1, pp. 272-280. Paisant L. 117, pp. 438-46.
88 Apparently, the two servants are not counted, nor is there mention of whether they are enslaved or free; see Appendix 2.

to the captain, and each tries to give us the best morsels of food. Finally, we must receive new compliments at every moment. They tell us unceasingly, "We love you very much, Madams, your manners toward everyone give us a good impression of your Institute." Another says: "I love to see you laugh, you laugh from your heart." And to me: "You are a good sailor, but you will remember Cape Finisterre[89] for a long time." It was there that I experienced the greatest fright.

They love Sister Xavier very much, above all, the captain, who tells her his successes and losses and the whole story of his life and that of his family. He is an admirable man; we have nothing but regret that he is Protestant; he has all the moral virtues. We do not give up hope of claiming him. Sister Xavier speaks to him from time to time. He loves the Catholic religion very much, but he has a prejudice against Catholics that it will be difficult to counter, having seen the horrors committed by the Spanish Catholics of Cuba. They have given him such a bad idea that it will be difficult to change it.

We also had several little discussions with another Protestant. He told me that he would be Catholic if it were not necessary to go to confession, but he did not wish to discuss this again. He always seeks us out; he always finds us happy and our happiness troubles him. Grace urges him, and I do not know if he will respond. After he had spoken for a long time with Sister Xavier, she said to him: "Know, sir, that you will not be happy and peaceful until you are a Catholic." That thought tormented him all day; he remained in a corner reflecting, and in the evening, he approached me and asked if I was never worried: "No, sir, never, since I belong to God." He asked us permission to come to see

---

[89] The north westernmost point of Spain, thus the last part of continental Europe. We are left uninformed of events there, also referred to in her journal for December 23.

us at the Ursulines. If he becomes Catholic, he will not be half-hearted. He says to me sometimes: "Is it necessary for me to be a priest or monk?" "No, sir, be a good Catholic in the world; God will not ask more of you."

We spend our days on deck with no difficulty, having such good fellow passengers. There we can make our meditation, our reading, and say office; after that we work. We always have Mrs. Chapela with us [the passenger who was ill]. We often recommend some little things to these gentlemen. That pleases them and has given them an entirely different idea of religious than they had before, the captain especially. When told that he would have religious on board, he believed that he would have to do more for them than for the other passengers. He got many expensive provisions, and so we have been too well treated. When he saw that we eat little and everything, he did not know what to think. Finally, one evening when we were on deck, he put his trust in Sister Xavier and asked her many questions about our Institute. He is educated and knows the Bible, so she instructed him and said: "Do you know the evangelical counsels?" "Yes, Madam." "Do you know the passage of the Gospel where Our Lord says to the young man, 'If you wish to be perfect go, sell what you have and give it to the poor, etc.?' That is what religious do, they embrace poverty by choice, obedience, and chastity." Since then he conceived a high idea of us and said to her, "I had formed a completely different idea of religious." He likes us very much and tries to give us pleasure, even coming to tell us when the sun is rising, because it is a charming sight when it appears on the horizon; in the evening he has us observe the sunset. He is teaching me to speak English, etc.

Well, Mother, I do not know how to tell you how good these gentlemen are to us, continually bringing us figs, prunes, etc. It seems that we are their children; we live in a family. One also sees Sister Xavier busy mending their suits, vests, ties, hats, caps; I sometimes do it and we do as much as we can since we see that it makes religion loved and gives a good idea of our Institute to the good Louisianians.

We have taken Mr. Nagliss for our mentor. He is an Irishman from Cork, a good friend of Sister Xavier. He is a man of great merit and quite devoted. He lives in Philadelphia and would really like a house of our order there, and I believe he will do all he can to have us. He promises us two young girls, daughters of one of his friends, for the house in Opelousas.

We often have little surprises that make us laugh unto tears; our gaiety edifies them and they come to tell us: "You are so happy, Madams, your lot is worthy of envy! Don't you have any worries?" I reply: "No, sir, since I am God's; never was I more free than since I gave up my liberty."

Finally, it is time to begin my journal.

**December 6th** at three in the afternoon, we embarked on the ship.

**Friday, December 7th** at three in the morning, the ship sailed and when we awoke I asked if we were still at Pauillac, and heard the response: "We are ten leagues away." My heart began to palpitate; I felt a great sorrow at leaving France. I would not have believed it, never having had that thought, but our good Master wished to use it for his glory; I made a generous sacrifice at once. The day was very beautiful.

**Saturday, December 8th** the same. We are at sea; I was the first to be sick and obliged to leave the table. We passed the day on the deck in order not to be sick.

**Sunday, December 9th** seasickness continues. Beautiful weather, we are making good progress. At night, all were sick; bad weather; I began to be frightened; I trembled during part of the night.

**Monday, December 10th** contrary winds; the sea is extremely high, but it is in our favor, otherwise there would have been much to fear. I was seasick and terrified. Mother Xavier is less suffering and has no fear; on the contrary, she is very happy with the noise and this furious sea.

**Tuesday, December 11th** the same. The **12th** even worse weather. No one can go on the deck except the sailors. The sea struck the sides at every moment; a wave came up to the window of the cabin where I was sitting. I was covered with water; at that moment, I thought I was drowning. Never will I forget the day of the 12$^{th}$, and the night; every time I saw the captain I asked for news of the weather: "Bad, Madam, bad; but do not fear, there is no danger." Finally, during the night, I thought I heard "danger" – "What is that?!" He laughed at my fear and said to me: "No danger; sleep, Madam, sleep."

**13th** contrary winds. We are not making progress; then the night was even worse. The ship stopped. Then strong rolling; one heard glasses and cups breaking on all sides, and even the chamber pots were knocked over on the gentlemen; I laughed a lot at that event.

**Friday, the 14th** contrary wind, rough sea, the captain restless; the seasickness continued. I began to fear no longer. At four in the evening, a good wind came: great joy, the dinner bell sounded. The captain came to get me saying: "Good wind, Madam, good wind."

**Saturday, the 15th** good wind; we made two and a half leagues an hour, strong rolling.

**Sunday, the 16th** contrary wind, sea very strong. **Monday the 17th** the same.

**Tuesday, the 18th** still worse, the contrary wind increased during several hours; we were ready to perish at any moment; I suffered very much that day and said: "Ah! If our mothers knew what we are suffering, they would be praying for us!" But I had recourse to the Heart of Jesus, and I was helped in a striking manner by the intercession of Aloysia.[90]

**Wednesday, the 19th** beautiful weather, good wind; we made sixty leagues that day.

**Thursday, the 20th** good wind, but the sea was calm.

**Friday, the 21st** calm sea, we do not make progress. We began to recover from seasickness; it had lasted twelve days.

**Saturday, the 22nd** contrary wind. **Sunday the 23rd** contrary wind; it increased at each moment. I am no longer afraid, I laugh at my fears, and they often speak to me of Cape Finisterre. I say that I will never forget it.

**Monday, the 24th** very strong contrary wind. People are beginning to murmur; only the captain remains tranquil. He is an admirable man; he is a lesson to us, even though he is Protestant.

**Tuesday, the 25th** contrary wind and a frightening night. **Wednesday, the 26th** The Lord came to our aid; good wind, good weather, all are rejoicing, we are making two and a half leagues an hour.

**Thursday, the 27th** good weather; today we saw the Canary Islands: a cry of joy; they came to wake us up to see the land. At eight in the morning we were opposite the town of Santa Cruz; on the other side we saw the peak of Tenerife, it is amazing to

---

90 Aloysia Jouve, Philippine Duchesne's niece, entered the Society and hoped to be a missionary like her aunt, but she died January 21, 1821, soon after her profession. She was considered by all to be very holy.

see that height of land in the midst of the vast ocean; it was visible all day. It was the feast of Saint John when I began to enjoy the trip. This day we passed between the Canary Islands and the Trinity [?]. These were the first we saw. We did not see Madeira, having passed it during the night.

**Friday** beautiful weather, good wind, two and a half leagues an hour. **Saturday the 29th** The same; we entered into the trade winds.

**Sunday, the 30th** at one o'clock we passed the Tropic, the heat is beginning and increases every day.

**Monday, the 31st** the good wind continues. Once we reached the trade winds, there is always good wind and there is only a calm to fear.

**Tuesday, January 1st** good weather; the wishes for the New Year are the continuation of the good wind.

**Wednesday, the 2nd** the good weather continues. We see a dolphin that swims around the ship. It amuses itself by making itself visible. It is a good twenty feet long; when it is under the water it appears azure blue.

**January 3rd** good weather; we make only two leagues an hour.

**Friday, the 4th** the same. **Saturday, 5th** the same. **Sunday, 6th** the same. **Monday, 7th** the same. **The 9th** same. **The 10th** calm weather. **11th** same. **12th** same. **13th** good wind. We saw a ship bound for Guadaloupe. We are opposite that island. **14th** calm. **15th** Good wind; we make two and a half leagues per hour.

**16th** we make only two leagues, and begin to see the island of Saint-Dominique; the heat is excessive. We are obliged to leave the door of our cabin open at night.

**17th** we make three leagues an hour. **18th** the same; at seven in the morning, we see the island of Cuba. **19th** beautiful weather. **20th** calm; we see a ship coming from Philadelphia; we speak to it with a horn. **21st** calm. **22nd** contrary wind that slows us down. We make only one league an hour. **23rd** calm. **24th** the same; contrary wind in the evening.

**25th,** feast of the Conversion of St. Paul, a day forever memorable because of the sad event that happened, but by the grace of God it was only a fright. The contrary wind during the night had pushed us too near the land of Cape Saint Anthony[91]; toward ten o'clock in the morning, we saw coming toward us a small rowboat of Spanish pirates. They were easily thirty armed people; they had guns and we did not. They rowed forcefully and we were becalmed. We could only wait to fall into their hands, if the Lord had not been our help. They raised the Spanish flag; we the American. They also raised an American flag; we had to depend on ourselves. All the sails were raised in order to go more quickly and to put out to sea because they did not leave the shores. Nevertheless, they gained on us and gave us a sign that declared war; we did not respond to them because we saw ourselves as taken. They were a quarter league from us. Everyone immediately began to hide money, the silver tableware, watches, etc. Everyone was frightened, trying to make arrangements with them so that they would not do us harm; we were ready to give them whatever they wanted provided they spared our lives. Finally, someone said: "If a good wind came, a great breeze, we would not need to fear them." I immediately threw myself at the feet of the Blessed Virgin to obtain by her intercession and that of Aloysia, the grace of a good wind and to deliver us from these pirates.

Immediately I was heard: a strong wind came, a good breeze that was against them and took us beyond them. They were

---

91 Cabo San Antonio, the westernmost point of Cuba.

obliged to turn back. What joy for all of us! How much I have thanked the Heart of Jesus, Mary, my good mother, and Aloysia. These gentlemen also cried: "It is only God who could have delivered us from such great danger. We would have preferred shipwreck rather than to fall into their hands." Others said: "How can we thank God? The grace is too great, it silences us, it is impossible for us to express in words."

This is what happened that day. As for us, we were calm, tranquil, we laughed a lot and you see that the Lord came to our rescue. As I obtained that grace through the intercession of Aloysia, I promised that I would tell you and give you all the details.

**26th** good wind, beautiful weather; we entered the Gulf of Mexico. **27th** good wind, but very little. **28th** the same. **29th** fog, which prevented us from seeing the land of America; we did not run aground; it seemed unavoidable any moment, but the Lord again came to our aid; they were able to anchor the ship, and we remained there until ten o'clock the next day. The pilot saw us and came to get us.

**30th** we are at the mouth of the Mississippi, but the wind is against us; we cast anchor to await a good wind. The pilot told us that the same pirates that we had seen, and from whom the Lord delivered us through the intercession of Aloysia, had a few days earlier taken an American ship. They had hanged the captain as well as the second in command, but they released the latter before he died and he was saved. They had shot the dining steward, then took everything that was on the ship; they left nothing, neither clothing nor food. All the men said: "We got out of there only by a miracle." They attributed this to our prayers, and we to Our Lady and Aloysia.

**31st** we are still at the mouth of the river; impossible to go up river.

**February 1st** a steamboat came from New York; seeing that the ship could be here a fortnight, we decided, as did all the passengers, to take the steamboat to go up river.

**February 2nd** we arrived in New Orleans at ten in the morning. Our good Mr. Nagliss, our mentor, took us quickly to the Ursuline sisters, who received us like their children. They were endlessly kind; we were overwhelmed by their care, by their foresight. Sister Xavier's soul is filled with joy; she has found several of these nuns who speak English. The Bishop [Dubourg], who happens to be here, came to see us an hour after our arrival. What joy to see that respected prelate! He quickly told us our destinations: "Sister Xavier, you are for Opelousas and Sister Lucile, I will take you with me to Florissant." I felt a great sorrow to be separated from my good Sister Xavier. It seemed to be Paul and Barnabas who were separated, if I can make that comparison, though we are far from them.[92] I will remain here more than a month to await the trip. Sister Xavier will leave at the first opportunity for Opelousas.

We are in very good health. America is our element. I am enchanted by the Americans; and I cannot pass over in silence that though we remained in the steamboat for twenty-four hours with more than fifty persons, we did not hear a single swearword. I admired their silence; if they spoke, it was very quietly, with propriety, with refinement. They are amused with a nothing; they gave us much polite attention. When we entered the room, all rose, someone brought us a stool, another oranges, pineapples, etc. We had the first places at table everywhere. On the steamboat, they said the grace aloud; all were standing with

---

92 Acts 15:39.

their hats off. It was the captain who led the grace, but in the Protestant version; we said it as Catholics. I regretted that these good men, so perfect in their religion, were not Catholics.

**Sunday, February 3rd** Bishop [Dubourg] preached in our chapel. There were many people. I admired the silence in the chapel. In the evening at five o'clock, it was full of young people and above all the Negroes. The rosary was said and all responded with such great fervor that I could not keep back my tears. I think that never in my life have I said my rosary so well. Afterwards the religious intoned a hymn, the congregation sang with us with all their heart, and I sang with all my voice and all my soul. The blessing followed; they remained a long time after in prayer. What is good here is very good, but there are the two extremes.

We just saw Father Martial a moment ago.[93] He told us that it is necessary to have more than supernatural prudence; one cannot say from the pulpit all that one wishes. New Orleans is a true Sodom, but it is not the same in Saint Louis. When one preaches to Catholics, they leave the church; immediately it is full of Protestants to whom he preaches in English. When they leave, they say: "What he tells us is very true."

---

93 Father Bertrand Martial, a secular priest, accompanied Philippine Duchesne and her companions on the *Rebecca* in 1818. Born in Bordeaux in 1770, he exercised his ministry in Saint Louis and New Orleans, where he died in 1832.

## 2. First Account of the Foundation at Sugar Creek, by Lucile Mathevon

French autograph, USCA

*[Note in another hand:]* Written by Mother Mathevon herself

Beginning of the Indian Mission by the Religious of the Sacred Heart, departed from St. Louis the 29$^{th}$ of June 1841, Philippine Duchesne, Lucile Mathevon, Mary A O'Connor, Louise Amiote, accompanied by the Reverend Fathers Verhaegen, Smedts, and Reverend Mr. Lecuillier. Our reception was beyond our expectations. Father Alen (Aelen) had made all the Indians assemble, men, women, and children, all in procession. At two miles from our habitation, they accompanied us. The women said their rosary. A *métis* named Joseph Bourrasa addressed us with a beautiful discourse in the name of the whole nation assembled to the number of 700, how happy they were to receive us to instruct their daughters in the true religion. I do not remember everything that Father Verhaegen answered to the Indians, that here is a woman who had asked God to come to teach them for 30 years, and that she was happy that God had given her this grace. Then everyone came to touch us on the hand, and Mother Duchesne embraced all the women and girls, and all the men gave us their hand. A great dinner was prepared at the home of Mr. Joseph Bertrand, a respectable *métis* whom we regarded as our benefactor. He is devoted to our Society unto death. Since Father Alene (Aelen) was not informed that we would arrive so early, he had not built a house. A good Indian named Manope loaned us his cabin that was below the church and lived in a tent for the 3 months that we stayed. The house could have been 15 feet long and 12 wide, and that is where we began the Indian school on July 19, 1841. The number of children became too many, all would not fit, so they made a path with tree branches. But since it was so easy for this man's chickens and turkeys, they came to perch, and every morning Mother O'Connor had to clean her classroom. When it rained, we had only the room I described above to have class for 50 girls, cook, sleep. 2 chairs, one for Mother Duchesne, who had her desk under her chair, and that was the whole size of her room. That is what she wrote to our Reverend Mother Foundress, with the joy of being able to practice poverty. We were very happy [p. 2] and gay. The government gave rations to the Indians of lard and corn flour. They brought us ours, too. We made a fire outside. It was not unusual to see when we arrived from church that the Indians' dogs had carried away our bread, even though it was well covered and with fire above it. They pulled it off with their paws, and our breakfast had to wait until more bread was baked. Sister Louise cut a piece of ham, and when she turned her back, a dog got it. The Indian Manope ran after it and so did we. He ran faster but could not catch it. We had 2 neighboring families who paid us much attention and went to get water in the woods for their children and as much as we needed. Father Allen (Aelen) had a good garden and we had vegetables. He gave us 4 cows. Reverend Mother Duchesne stayed all morning in the church, and Sister Louise brought her a cup of coffee at the door of the church. After dinner, she stayed 3 or 4 hours in the church. The Indians had great respect for her. They recommended themselves to her prayers and called her the lady who always prays. They missed her very much. I think that through her prayers, a great number were baptized. Every Sunday there were 3 or 4 men or women with their whole family who were baptized. She wrote all their names, which edified us very much. When they encountered us going to the church, they made the sign of the cross and knelt to ask our blessing. Afterwards, they gave us their hand. We were much edified to see every Sunday 300 or 400 receive communion. I would raise my head and I would see the sacred host leave the hands of Father Veyete (Verreydt) and go to rest on the tongue of a good woman in the crowd. I cannot distinguish in such a way as to know the name, but the father knows. But another good Indian named Queguen told me that one day he went on a journey. He thought about the passion of Our Lord. He heard behind him a sort of voice that told him the whole passion. He was a man very interior and spiritual. He instructed the other Indians every Sunday. He led them under a tree, and there for 2 hours he taught the catechism with them. There was another named Pokeguen. He taught the catechism in the church for the girls and boys after Mass. At the end, his recommendations were that we must respect our fathers and love our mothers.

[p. 3] Our house was soon built, one room and an attic where we slept. In winter, the snow fell on us. We put up a tent, 3 under the tent. The floor was in *clabor* [clapboard] one on the other as on the roof, so that our bed was not vulnerable, and the snow was on the side and had to be removed every morning. And it was in such a room that we received our Very Reverend Mother Galitzine. So we had a bed to offer her. All the Indians the next morning came in procession to greet our reverend mother. Mr. Joseph Bourassa gave her a fine discourse. Afterwards, our mother, seeing all the women bringing her their children, caressed them, saying, "Yes, little one, you have a dirty nose," and these good women thought that they were beautiful compliments that she gave them. We laughed heartily. We had the visit of Bishop Kennerick [Kenrick], archbishop of St. Louis. He confirmed 280 Indians. The same day, 200 received the scapular. We always had 80 girls in the school. Sometime later, we had 15 boarders. The parents sent us goat meat, rabbits, squirrels, and tender corn that they prepare dry, and we gave soup to everyone. The day students could not stay all day without eating anything. Many learned to read well and to write numbers and do needlework. Some sewed and others carded wool and cotton and knitted stockings. When the Superintendent from St. Louis, Mr. Mitchel, [visited] one of our little Indian girls carded and knitted a pair of slippers. The Superintendent was very satisfied and gave her a *piastre*. He took them with him and said that he would show them in Washington. However, during the 7 years that we stayed at Sugar Creek, we received nothing from the government except the last year, we had a good agent, Mr. Vane. He gave us 80 *piastres*. I do not remember receiving anything else. Father Veryete (Verreydt) gave us everything we needed for food. Mother Duchesne received 200 *piastres* with which we had a room built, and there was a passageway between these two wooden buildings. Then we were better lodged. We had a house for the provisions and a little cabin to wash the laundry, a beautiful garden, many chickens, 10 cows. We had a domestic who worked with Father Nails (Neal), a *cueil lait* (curds?), much corn. We had the visit of Reverend Mother Cutts, who brought with her Sister Mary Layton and took Mother Thiefry, who remained as superior for two years. We had the visit of Bishop Barron. He confirmed a great number. A great number were children whom we had instructed, [p. 4] most of these girls [now at] Saint Marys, and we teach their children at present. Others are dead, and had an edifying death. One converted her whole family, another her mother, a good Indian [when] about to die, called for the father. The one who spoke Indian was not at home. Another went. He took his notebook in which were written sins in Indian language. But the good Indian, who lived in such a saintly way, said to him: "Father, my sins are not in your notebook." The father knew her and gave her absolution. After staying 7 years at Sugar Creek, the government wanted to move our Indians. We did not know if our mother general would allow us to move. Nevertheless, our Indians did not want to abandon us. All the chiefs came, and one told us his thoughts. He said, "What a sad thought to leave you behind us. Come, mothers, we will take care of you." Then I wrote to Reverend Mother Barat, our general. Father Vereyte [Verreydt] also wrote to her and we made a novena to St. Francis Xavier and to the archangel Gabriel. On the last day of the novena, we learned that it was that very day that reverend mother general approved our move. We waited 9 months doing nothing, waiting for our Indians to be relocated. They did not want to cross the Kansas River. Finally, Father Verreydt came to choose the place, and Mr. Bertrand chose where we are at present, finding the ground good and a little creek. He said, here is a garden for Mother O'Connor and water for her cows and calves. They built us a little house. It had 2 rooms. There we began the Indian school on September 9, 1848. We then had to take boarders to keep them from going to the Protestants. The Baptist mission had begun before us. 8 days later, we had 15. They slept in a little attic where one could not stand up straight. 3 slept in the other room. We had class in the morning and Mass. Finally after 2 months they built a little chapel that we use now to store corn. During this time, they built a 2 story house and the church. When we arrived here, it was a vast prairie where there were never any inhabitants. It was a place for the buffalo. The land had never been cultivated, and now it is inhabited by up to 200 thousand or more. In the first years, we had 50 boarders and they increased every year to about 90.

## 3. Second Account of the Foundation at Sugar Creek, by Lucile Mathevon

French autograph, USCA

Journal of the foundation of the house of the Sacred Heart
At Sugar Creek Indian Territory

*[In another hand, English:]* In M Mathevon's own hand

The Religious of the Sacred Heart left in the number of 4 for the mission of the Potovoitomise [sic] Indians at Sugar Creek. Mother Lucille Mathevon, superior, Mother Philippine Duchesne, Mother Mary Anne O'Connor and Sister Louise Amiote, all professed. We left St. Louis June 29, 1841, to get on the steamboat named *Emilie* accompanied by Bishop Lachanse, bishop of Nathes [sic],[94] of Reverend F. Vendevelde, president of the University of St. Louis, of F. Renaud, priest of the cathedral of St. Louis, of Misters Kelly, benefactor of the establishment, Mr. Borne Demies Fortune Wolche, of Mrs. McLaughline Amon Wolche, and the Misses Murphy Fortune McKeys, all benefactors of this establishment. After having received the apostolic blessing and thanked our friends for all their kindness, we stayed with our dear Father and founder of this establishment, Reverend Father Verhaegen, Provincial of the Jesuits of Missouri and always our father and protector of this establishment. Having asked our Reverend Mother Provincial de Galitzine to begin this important mission and having consented, she named the father provincial superior and told me to leave when he would tell us. Nevertheless, this good mother, not

---
94  John-Marie Chance, S.S., bishop of Natchez 1840-1852.

knowing where she was sending us, had some fears and wanted a delay; but our good Father Verhaegen with his great courage and unlimited confidence in God came to tell me that we must leave, because Providence will take care of everything, and I will help you. [p. 2] So the next week we left. We had to go get Mother O'Connor at St. Charles. There Mother Hamilton wanted to oppose her departure and told him, I have no one to replace her. But [he] cut her short and said this is not my business, prepare everything. That dear mother did not dare say another word and he brought her to St. Louis. So there we were all together. I prepared the packets and purchased our little *ménage*: marmite, stove for warmth, pot, coffee maker, and provisions of sugar, coffee, rice, molasses, crackers, flour, stove for cooking, tools for working the ground and the carpentry, in sum, everything needed in a region where one finds little to buy of these sorts of things.

So we departed accompanied by good Father Verhaegen, superior, Smedts and Father Renaud, priest of the cathedral, and a Negro named Edmond whom Mother de Galtizine gave us. These good fathers were full of kindness toward us. We were very well treated on the steamboat by Captain Cuser and his wife, who sought to be instructed in our holy religion. The first three days we saw a great quantity of towns along the banks of the Missouri. The most populated were Jefferson and Bonne Ville, this last one well built up and with more than 6,000 inhabitants. They wanted us to make an establishment in that town, where there is no one to teach the young. But that was not our purpose. Our hearts were rent to see so many people without priests, without churches, without schools. There were more towns and habitations all along the river, without knowledge of our holy religion. There were a few abandoned Catholics in each town who wanted priests. But the harvest is abundant and there are few workers. In passing, our fathers baptized several children. [p. 3] On the third day we celebrated July 4 at three o'clock in the afternoon. They arranged in the grand room of the steamboat a table furnished with white wine and other liquor, the chairs in a row, all the gentlemen of the steamboat, to the number of more than 50, together in great silence. They went to get Reverend Father Verhaegen, who delivered a sermon appropriate for the solemnity of the day. Everyone applauded in the American style with hands and feet. Afterwards, they presented chilled wines and we drank to the health of the good father and of Washington. Afterwards, the fathers amused themselves with the gentlemen like little children. We had 20 soldiers who were going to the fort. They had a tambourine and a clarinet. They played almost as if to make bears dance. This entertained us all evening on July 4. We disembarked and were at the house of Mrs. Chouteau that is on the riverbank 5 miles from Westport. All our effects were carried there. This good lady received us with so much goodness and charity. We spent Sunday with her. Since we arrived early, Father Verhaegen sent Father Renaud to say Mass at the church of Westport that is 2 miles from the house of Mrs. Chouteau. He rang the bell but since he did not know anyone, and not knowing the customs of the area, seeing that no one came, he returned without saying Mass. As soon as the town knew that there had been a priest, 40 or 50 people came, very upset that they had not arrived in time to have Mass. They came all the way to Mrs. Chouteau's house to see the fathers and asked for a priest from the superior who [p. 4] at the same time represented the bishop during his absence among them. As soon as he heard it, Father Verhaegen joked with Father Renaud all along the way and reproached him for having committed 40 venial sins for having made these great people miss Mass. Father Renaud, a simple man of good and delicate conscience, said so sweetly and contritely, "I am truly sorry, I am truly sorry." This amused us very much. At 5 in the morning, Father Renaud said Holy Mass at the home of Mrs. Chouteau, and we had the happiness to receive Communion as well as the good fathers. After breakfast, Mrs. Chouteau prepared for us everything she thought would be necessary to make 70 miles on land where we would not find habitations.

There were immense prairies that we had to cross. Two large *Waigaines* arrived from Westport, one for the fathers and one for us. We got in and arrived at Westport two hours after noon, and we stopped with a good family where we were well received and they gave us a good dinner. We purchased several things for our journey, among others 50 loaves of bread that the baker made while we were dining. At about 4 o'clock we got on the road, but it was too late to get to a habitation. When we arrived at a beautiful river, we camped and there they lit a great fire, and we made coffee, and with ham we had supper on the grass under the trees. Afterwards, our evening was one of the most pleasant and funny that I have ever seen in my life. The fathers stretched out some wool blankets and lay down on them. Father Verhaegen could not sleep and talked all night. The next day he asked me if he was too talkative. I answered that I had never seen such a babbler. [p. 5] He kept us from sleeping. But that wasn't all. They had not tied the horses well enough, and the drivers were sleeping. Two got away, and we had to stay half a day while they looked for them, which disturbed our whole route and obliged us to sleep 2 more nights in the prairie, and do our own cooking like the Indians and take our meat in our two hands without plates, drink one after the other. But all of this was very amusing. I had never had a journey so enjoyable, so happy. Father Allen [Aelen], superior of the Potawatomi Indian Mission, came ahead of us at the 21st mile. What joy to see this good father again. How he received us with his usual affability. Finally he was ready to go to a habitation where he had been waiting for us since the day before, where he had prepared everything to receive us. These are some French people who have a store to sell to the Indians of different nations who come there. This house is situated on the Osage River. There are many troublesome Indians of that nation there known by the whites. This good Mr. Girou received us very well and gave us his bedroom. We spent a very enjoyable evening there. In the evening, Father Verhaegen went to fish in the Osage River. Afterwards, the Indians went there with torches and got us fish for breakfast the next day, July 10, which was a Friday. Since Father Aelen had assembled the whole village to receive us, they stayed all day in the prairie, impatient to see us. 2 Indians came 18 miles. They arrived at 9 o'clock in the evening. As soon as they saw Father Verhaegen, they fell to their knees [p. 6] to ask his blessing and to learn if we had arrived. They were told yes. They left and went back during the night to inform the others all the length of the route, 2 by two Indians mounted on beautiful horses came in front of us every 2 or 3 miles. We found two to greet us and they got off their horses to ask the blessing of the great father. Since he held the place of the bishop, they addressed him that way. Finally when we arrived 1 mile from the house of Father Aelen, we found the whole village in procession coming in front of us, arranged in perfect order, the 2 fathers Aelen and Eysvogels on horseback with their square hats, the chief of the Indians, 2 children carrying two flags, one white with a red cross and stars, the other red. All were on horseback. Following were 150 mounted Indians in their best dress, the horses well harnessed. After, about 300 men with rifles followed, then the men on foot, the women, girls, and boys. There were 6 flags, all in the best order. For our welcome, 2 Indians took the bridles of our horses and held them this way during the discharge of rifles. Then the cavalry lined up on both sides of our wagons, and they advanced our wagons this way through the middle of the cavalry, then they made semi-circles around us, then half crescents in perfect order. Not a single horse's foot advanced farther than another. The women said their rosary. When we arrived near the house of Reverend Father Aelen, they had us get down from the wagon and sit on prepared benches. 5 Jesuit fathers, 4 Religious of the Sacred Heart, all the Indians arranged in 4 lines around us in the most perfect order. Then the chief approached us and greeted us. What happiness for us, we see these religious arrive to instruct our children in the true religion. It was all resaid to us by the interpreter. After, the chief's wife also did hers about the same, and she added, for proof of our joy, all our girls will shake your hand. Then 2 girls [p. 7] approached us and presented to Mother Duchesne 2 images, one of the Sacred Heart of Jesus and the other of Mary. Then Reverend Father Verhaegen addressed them some words, saying that he had traveled well in the United States, but had never seen such a reception with such order, and that he was very satisfied. Then he told them, here is a lady of 73 who has wanted to come for 30 years to instruct the Indians, that she was filled with joy to see her desires accomplished. Then he said that these religious had come for their spiritual and temporal happiness. Then we went to the church followed by a crowd of Indians. Then they took us to the house of Mr. Bertrand, the chief figure of the village, who has an American wife, the most amiable that I have known. We were well received. She had prepared a good dinner both fat and lean. It was a Friday. For the first time in my life, I ate meat on Friday out of obedience to Reverend Father Verhaegen, who gave the permission taking the place of the bishop, and in a country where one does not find everything. Since the house was not ready, they rented the house of an Indian. It is a log house 18 feet long and 12 wide. That is where they brought us. It is situated below the church, in a pretty place. We were surrounded by Indians, but great people who sing continually the praise of God. On Saturday, July 11, we had 3 Masses. Father Aelen heard confessions all day and the evening until 11 o'clock in the evening. On the 12$^{th}$ at the first Mass that Father Verhaegen said, there were 150 Communions. They sang the Mass at 10 o'clock with music. I have never heard such beautiful singing and music so well played. After Mass the father superior gave baptism to 4 adults. The Indians sang vespers for two hours in their language and they do it like that every Sunday. We were edified to see such piety in this parish of Indians who were only infidels 5 years ago. There are 1,000 Catholics. Father Hoken [Hoecken] came first. After much trouble and effort, he baptized 400. Reverend Father Aelen came in 1839 to take his place. He knew how to gain the confidence of all the Indians, learned their language, and he won all the rest for God. He put perfect order in the parish, because he is persuaded that to keep them in fervor he had to establish frequent confession and [p. 8] Communion. He has them approach the holy table every month. If he sees someone who delayed, he only has to say, you must come to confession. They answer, what day? Now, he answers. They follow the priest and go to confession. Every morning more than 100 assist at the Holy Mass, and they sing hymns in their language. Before Mass an Indian leads the prayer aloud. After the Mass he asks for the catechism lesson with the children, boys and girls. There are always more than 30 of one or the other in the evening in the chapel. They ring the bell for evening prayer and they assist. Every Sunday there are more than 100 at the holy table. Reverend Father Herman Aelen has done the greatest good here and has been ready to give his life for his flock. One day there was a party among the Potawatomi nation who had not yet returned to God. They are almost always enemies, and so very bad. Seeing that they wanted to kill some women and girls, he put himself there to defend them and the good God took care of his days. 3 times they wanted to kill him with a saber and 3 times the moon reflected on his belt buckle. He was calumniated, saying that he had enemies. I declare that he did not have any except those who are enemies of God. He is loved and respected by the whole flock. To see a young Jesuit priest sacrifice everything and to have no one for company but wretched Indians, he is like the father of all and they are like little children around their father. I saw him one Sunday just after vespers in his sacristy surrounded by his dear Indians, all the men already advanced in age, telling them stories, speaking to them and laughing with them. It was admirable.

On July 15 he went to do a mission with the Osage Indians. He stayed there 4 days. During that time he lived on roots like the Indians. He was well received by the chief. He preached to them; and while they listened with great attention, someone stole the bridle of his horse, but the chief made him give it back. He baptized 50 people, several of them adults. He told them that the Potawatomis had some religious to instruct their daughters. The chief said that he would certainly like to have some, but while waiting, he would send their daughters here; and for proof of his affection for us, he sent us 5 *piastres* to help build our house. The converted Indians prayed for the conversion of the other Indians. It was July 18, 1841, that the father returned from the Osage and that I received their money.

[p. 9] On July 19, 1841, memorable day when we began the Indian school at Sugar Creek, there were 12 the first day and second day 42, the third day 50, and every day that continues, 50 to 60 girls and women who come to learn to read, work. We have holy Mass every day, where the father preaches. On July 22, feast day of our reverend mother (Barat), was the first feast day that we had here. We had a joyful recreation. We made tarts and sent some to the father. We spent all the rest of the time very joyful and happy in the joy of the Lord for having been chosen for this dear mission even though very unworthy. We are poorly lodged and fed the same way and that is the subject of our joy and our great contentment, sleeping on a wooden Indian bed. That is where we sleep more than in a royal palace. We are awakened at 4 o'clock in the morning by the chickens who come down from the trees and sit on our roof, which makes a good wakeup call. Some lard, a cup of coffee, corn bread, that is our good breakfast every day. At dinner, lard, rice soup, pumpkin butter, white cheese drained. That is our good dinner. On July 31, 1841, feast of St. Ignatius Loyola, we had high Mass, a beautiful panegyric of St. Ignatius at the Mass, many people. The night before, I said to Father Aelen that we are also the daughters of St. Ignatius because we have the same rules. He joked by saying no. But in the morning I saw him in the sacristy after Mass and I said to him, "Father, I wish you a good feast of St. Ignatius." Then he answered with these words that went to the bottom of my heart: "I greet you, daughter of St. Ignatius." I asked this great saint to give me the spirit of our holy rules, and that he will give these dear children to work like them at our perfection by working for our neighbor. In the evening we had Benediction of the Blessed Sacrament. For the first time, we sang the litany of the Blessed Virgin, and my little Indian girls answered in Latin, *ora pro nobis*. We sang a hymn in Indian and in English. On August 1 there were 150 Communions, and on the second day, Mass and Communion. After that he left to go, to the greater glory of God, to a priest who he believed needed his ministry, to see this poor man and at the same time some Catholic families at a distance; and there he heard the confessions of the whole parish, put things in order, and empowered the priest.

[p. 10] 3 and 4 no Mass. The Indians cut wood to build our house.

5 No Mass. Father is on mission.

6 No Mass

8 Return from mission. Confession, Communion

All week he prepared 45 people for First Communion.

9, 10, 11 They carried wood for our house all day.

August 15, 1841, memorable day. There were 45 people who made their First Communion after having been prepared all week by 2 instructions a day, one in the morning and the other in the afternoon. The same day there were 250 people who received Communion. The evening before, the father heard confessions for 17 hours. He gave the scapular to 275 people, and having had to say that prayer so many times greatly tired him. Before the high Mass he baptized a man to whom he gave the name Herman. After the high Mass he did 2 marriages. Vespers were very solemn. There was exposition of the Blessed Sacrament. I sang the litany of the Blessed Virgin with my little Indian girls. We will never forget that day and the fatigue of good Father Aelen. He went at 11 o'clock in the evening to visit a sick person.

On Saturday vigil of the Assumption when he arrived he heard confessions until 2 hours before midnight. He remained in the confessional 17 hours. On August 18 he baptized 3 men of whom one was the brother of the chief of the Ottawa. On the 25th, all the Indians were employed building our house, and in 2 days the whole wooden frame was raised. We gave them a dinner: 3 cornbreads, pumpkin, and beans well flavored with lard. They were very happy. On the Sunday after Assumption, there were 50 Communions and 40 to whom the scapular was given. The Sunday of the Heart of Mary, 29th of August, there were 25 Communions. On the 28th, I received a letter from Father Verhaegen, the first I received since the 2 months that we have been here and one from Mother Shannon from Opelousas. The house was finished on October 9th, and we entered it that evening. All day the Indians had brought our baggage. The women and girls swept the house, and in a few hours everything had been brought. The chimney was not finished so we made a fire outside. One morning during Mass [p. 11] a dog stole the cover from the oven and carried off the bread.

October 15 I received a letter from our reverend mother general that gives me her happiness about this mission and naming me superior since she cannot come herself. She says that she envies my happiness. I was confused to have been chosen in the place of this reverend mother for this work that I hope will give glory to God. I came here with only that intention. Every day we have 15 to 18 children who come to class. On the 21st, they all left to go get the payment. The Indian who loaned us his house has left us his little daughter to care for. On the 24th, the fathers went with them to prevent drunkenness and quarrels. On Sunday, there was only one low Mass.

From this time it was Mother Duchesne who continued the journal.[95]

The bishop came to give Confirmation on June 15, 1842. He had 265 to confirm. He left June 20 and took Father Aelen to the great regret of all the Indians and of us. He was the father of the whole nation by his charity, goodness, exactitude, firmness that he held particularly for the Indians. Fathers Verreydt and Hoecken stayed and the young Hoecken, his brother, to learn the language. Mother Duchesne left here July 24 to stay in St. Charles. The school always continues. There are always 30 to 40 children. We have a beautiful garden. It is enough to nourish us with the milk of 5 cows.

Our new building was finished June 19 through the great care of Reverend Father Aelen who spared nothing to get it finished before his departure, as well as the field that he had worked. It was all finished before his departure.

On August 26 Brother Marcelli (Mazzella) went to St Louis. [p. 12] On August 28, 1842, many people received Communion. The first of October, all went to the (government?) payment. Everything went well there. They admired the Indians from Sugar Creek, their good appearance, their cleanliness. They paid their debts. On October 15, they left for the hunt. Our school continued, since during the hunt there were 25 each day.

On November 1, 1842, we had the visit of the superintendent of the Indians from St. Louis. He assisted at the Mass that was well celebrated with music and singing. He admired the tranquility that reigned. He visited our school. Several children

---

95 There is no change of handwriting here, and by the end of the paragraph, Mother Duchesne has gone.

read in front of him. He admired the progress of Marie [illegible name] in reading and needlework. He gave a *piastre* for the pair of stockings she had made, carding the wool and knitting the stockings, and he said inside a house that these stockings would be brought to Congress in Washington. He promised to get us 300 *piastres*.

On June 1, 1843, we had the visit of the Indian superintendent Mr. Mitchell. He made a second visit to us. We arranged our school nicely. There were 40 in the class. They had prepared sewing to show him. He was charmed to see an Indian class as good as among the whites. They read in front of him, recited verses, and sang in English and Latin. Then they presented their work. One had made a pair of shoes in the Indian fashion all embroidered that she offered to him. Another had made a pair of [illegible] embroidered in ribbon in Indian fashion that was offered to him, which he received with gratitude. The others showed him a little dress made by Angelique Michaba (or Michubu) a child of 11 years. Others made artificial flowers that they presented to him. He admired two surplices beautifully embroidered, 3 men's shirts, a pair of stockings, pants of wool and well carded cotton. He said to me right away, "Madame Lucille, you have a box?" I answered yes, and he told me to put everything in it. "I am going to take it all and send it to Washington. I am very satisfied. I will have you take the presents and put [p. 13] the name of the child who did the work and her age. They will be presents." He came to see us a second time to make notes of all the interest he took in our school and promised me 500 *piastres*. Reverend Father Verhaegen came at that moment with him and showed us great kindness. On the feast of Corpus Christi he had a procession with the Blessed Sacrament in a splendid manner.

The whole week was spent in preparation. A large flag of ten square feet with turbans for the army captains, the tables turned upside down for the expositions and the boxes of candles inside to do the exposition well. With the Indians he had prepared a beautiful repository. At last everything was in order and the procession was held on Sunday after vespers in admirable order.

From the year 1843 until 1845 on June 16 I [Lucile] take up the journal, having been removed from my charge and having been restored to it by Reverend Mother Cutts, our visitatrice, who came here May 26 with Reverend Father Van de Velde, provincial of the Jesuits. They left May 29 and took Mother Thiefry with Mother Xavier who both had stayed here 2 years.[96] Abundant rains prevented the children from coming to school. There were only 10 who came.

On June 24, Father Hoecken went to the hunt with a party of Indians. They made a camp where he said Mass every day. At the same time we received the news that the government will give us 500 *piastres* per year. One party of Indians [p. 14] went to the bluff where they made a treaty to change their land. The whole month of July was extremely hot. The number of children grew. They were 30 in the class. The chief of the Chippewa came to invite the fathers to visit his nation, as well as the Peoria and the Ottawa, and Father De Coen went on August 17 where they are to have a great council to unite themselves. They only want to have Catholic priests and to get rid of their ministers.

The cold began November 25. Winter was very cold and long.

---

96 No other Society document of the time records that during this two-year stay of Catherine Thiéfry that Lucile was removed from office. Catherine Thiéfry, RSCJ (1792-1867) was superior at Florissant when Mother Duchesne founded the City House, then changed places with her in 1834. Mother Xavier was Marie Xavier Ann Kavanagh (Cavanagh), born in Ireland and entered the Society in 1837. After she left Sugar Creek, there is no more record of her. She presumably left the Society then.

There were a few days of good weather before Christmas, and Father De Coen went to Westport to get Bishop Barron, coadjutor of Bishop Kenrick, bishop of St. Louis. It was a few days before Christmas, and he assisted at the midnight Mass, where he preached in English, and the Mass was sung with music. There were Indians from four nations, Potawatomi, Peoria, Ottawa, and Osage. The celebrations of Christmas were beautiful. The following Sunday he gave Confirmation to 80 Indians, of whom there were 12 of our children from the school. The good bishop showed us a great deal of interest and left very satisfied with our good Indians. The children had embroidered a surplice. It was given to him as a present. He was very satisfied. On January 26, we received the money promised by the government for the school. Since they talked about changing the Indians' lands, one for another larger one, he asked us if we would go, as some doubts were raised. If this change were to be made, he answered us, I cannot go without you. I cannot go by myself.

The whole month of January was good weather, and on February 12 a foot of snow fell. After that, the weather was very cold. Since the month of October to the present, more than one hundred children have died of whooping cough, more than 40 adults all of pleurisy or having taken cold. Father De Coen had whooping cough. There were very many ill this winter.

[p. 15] The establishment among the Potawatomi at the Kansas River began September 9, 1848.

We arrived 4 religious: Mother O'Connor, Sister Mary Layton, S Louise Amiotte, Lucille Mathevon, superior of this establishment. Father Verreydt, Father Galien arrived with us. Mr. Joseph Bertrand brought us. We had 5 vehicles of Indians who brought our effects. We made a dinner near the little river before arriving here. The 17th of September, day of the feast of

Our Lady of 7 Dolors, the first Mass that was ever said since J. C. was said that day by Father Verreydt. Afterwards they planted a cross on the highest point of the mountain that is behind our house. Everyday Mass was said in our room. The Indians arrived every day to be there.

Mr. Joseph Bertrand died November 6, 1848. He was our benefactor. He was the first who came to find this place and the first who was buried there. He did much for this mission. He died very peacefully, pronouncing the names of Jesus and Mary. He had great devotion to the Blessed Virgin. He wanted to give the name Our Lady of the Lake to this place. It was called simply St Mary, the town; the parish, St Joseph.

November 26, 2 boarders entered. Father Hoecken went to the hunt with the Indians. Several families arrived and built houses in the woods. He arrived January 13. It snowed November 3. This whole month was cold. On December 3, 1848, a great quantity of snow fell, such as we had not seen for a long time. There were two feet in place, the same on 3d and 4th. January 25, 1849, it began to disappear.

[p. 16] That day there was a great wind blowing snow, and it was extremely cold. By evening the ground was covered with ice.

## 4. Memories of Marie Monzert, RSCJ (after 1869)

French typed copy and English translation, GASSH

Notes on the Life of Mother Lucile

*[Handwritten marginal notes on English translation:]*
Written by M. R. Monzert or Julia Deegan, who arrived in 1868—see paper—probably Monzert, who like to write things up. In Roman archives – rscj

The first time that I saw Mother Lucile was in 1852, when she was bringing to St. Louis Sister Louise who was attacked by lung trouble to consult the doctors. She had had much to suffer on her long trip made in a cart-wagon travelling over land without roads, being obliged to traverse forests, immense prairies, over a country almost uninhabited. One day, the driver having strayed from the way and after wandering about during a whole day over the prairie, seeing night approach, he declared that he did not know where he was. Our travelers were very much frightened; but they had to resign themselves to pass the night under the beautiful stars, as it was impossible to discover a sign of human habitation. They spent the night in the cart, indeed, and their driver slept beneath. They let him sleep undisturbed, for they had discovered that he had with him a bottle of whiskey of which he had drunk too much. Mother Lucile covered the Sister the best she could and tried to make her rest, but for herself she prayed and begged Divine Providence all that long night to preserve them from savage beasts, which abounded in those parts.

They reached St. Joseph for the Feast of the Sacred Heart and were very well received by M. Scanlan, pastor of the parish, who brought them to the home of an old pupil of St. Louis. He was the only priest and he had no religious order as yet in his parish, (the town), which had been founded only a few years before. The pupils begged Mother Lucile very earnestly to interest Mother du Rousier in them and their cause, (They thought her then in St. Louis) and to obtain for them some religious of the Sacred Heart. She succeeded easily, and the foundation took place the following year. They finally reached St. Louis, after a journey of three weeks. The principal intention in going to St, Louis had been to see Reverend Mother Durousier [sic], but Mother Lucile did not have this consolation; for after waiting fifteen days, she had to return with a Reverend Jesuit Father, who could not wait any longer. So she was obliged to leave before the arrival of Rev. M. Durousier. A large number of people were made happy by seeing her during her sojourn in St. Louis, and they gave her many presents for her poor mission, for as yet they were not supported by the government and had for resources only what was given to them. They had, however, the wherewithal to feed and clothe almost eighty little Indians, who were not yet civilized and who were not attracted to us yet; and in spite of all we could do to tame them, they escaped our vigilance. It was not a rare occurrence after many hours of search to find twenty of them in the woods, sitting in a straight line in perfect order and perfectly tranquil; so that it was impossible to even make them change their positions, until the fancy took them, when they all left as if by enchantment and suddenly returned to the house. Sometimes one of the Jesuit Brothers was obliged to go out on horseback to look for them and to drive them back before him like a flock of sheep.

Later on when they were a little more "tamed," they did not escape in such large bands; but from time to time they left in small bands of three or four. They escaped one from one place, one from another, then met at an appointed place. The one that arrived first, waited for the others but never did they betray one another. In 1868, the 1st of February, three left us thus. It was the Mistress General's Feast; they had had recreation all day; it was frightful weather, a drizzly rain, which froze as it fell, made the ground so icy that it was almost impossible to walk. Towards evening without any reason for discontent these three small children, nine to ten years of age, escaped. Two of them lived twenty and the third, thirty miles from St. Mary's. They reached home the third day; their clothes, soaked from the rain, were entirely frozen. At the end of three weeks their parents brought them back to us, as if nothing had happened, and asked above all that they should not be punished. I cite the example as only one among a hundred because I was an eyewitness of this one.

The house or convent was built by the Indians with the trunks of trees, interwoven, and the cracks filled in with pieces of stone and mud; while this again in the interior was covered with cotton cloth, which swole out [sic] and rose and fell like the sails of a ship when the wind blew. There was no other floor than a few planks laid on the ground. Almost all the rooms were separated one from the other, so that to go to the refectory, to the vestry, to the infirmary, to the dormitory, one had to go through the yard exposed to the inclemency of the weather. When the parents came, whether to see their children, or for any other reason, they entered into our midst without even knocking at the door, and it seemed that we had to submit to this or we would otherwise hurt them.

When I came to St. Mary's, they gave me charge of a dormitory, and they told me not to worry about anything the first days but to pay attention to all that went on about me, that I might thus learn what I should do later. That morning I rose at half-past-four; when dressed, I knelt down to say my prayer, thinking I should have a good half-hour of meditation. But I had scarcely finished my morning prayer, when I heard a little noise. I did not pay any attention to it, thinking that it was not yet the hour of rising. At the end of a quarter of an hour, having turned around to see what was going on, what was my surprise to find myself all alone in a large empty room. All had disappeared: children, beds, etc. Their only toilet consisted in putting on a cotton dress, which was done in three minutes. Their bed was a mattress, a sheet, and a little quilted coverlet, stretched on the floor, which they had carried away on their backs and thrown over the fence to air. Then they went to get their shoes (which they did not wear in summer, except to go to church) and went to the study-hall for morning prayer. They went right after this to Holy Mass. Breakfast was a quarter of an hour later, and then two Mistresses took them for combing and washing (which had not taken place before, because of the early hour).

They did not have the happiness of having Holy Mass in the house, and they were obliged to go to the Parish Church for all their exercises of piety. To reach this they had to cross a yard more than fifty feet long. Mass was said and Holy Communion was given every day at a quarter to six; and in winter when it had snowed all night, it was very difficult to clear a path in the darkness. Thus they often reached the church with their shoes filled with snow, which of course melted on their feet during Mass.

The Church was made of the trunks of trees like the house, but instead of a floor it had only a few boards placed on the beams without even being nailed and so far apart that one could put ones' hands in the cracks. Bishop Miege passed the three first years of his episcopate at St. Mary's, and I have heard him say with his own lips that he had never suffered so from the cold as when saying Mass in this church. On one occasion amongst many others, he was so frozen that he lost consciousness, and they were obliged to carry him to his room, so that he could not finish Holy Mass.

When I was sent to St. Mary's in 1868, the church had been somewhat repaired: it had a stove, but it was still intensely cold. They had made a sort of road with broken stones to reach it; but when the ground was covered with snow and in the darkness, it was not a rare occurrence to step outside the path and to fall into the ditch.

In spite of all these difficulties and no matter how suffering, Mere Lucile never failed to go to Holy Mass, that is, if it were possible for her to rise at all; and her greatest sacrifice was always to be deprived of the happiness of assisting at the Holy Sacrifice, when the illness from which she suffered prevented her from rising (an illness of many years).

*N.B. The typed copy of the English translation bears page numbers 6, 7, and 8.*

## 5. Memories of Elizabeth Schrader, RSCJ (after 1879)

*English autograph, USCA*

S.C.J.M.

I, Mother Elizabeth Schroeder, desiring to fulfill Rev. Mother's wish that I should give an account of my story at St Mary's, Kansas, have written the following.

In the early part of the year 1856, I was very ill and the Community begged to make a novena to Mother Duchene [*sic*] for my recovery, making the promise in case that it was granted that I should go to the Indian Mission. Rev. Mother Jouve gave permission for the novena saying, as she left Grande [*sic*] Coteau at the beginning of April to make the regular visit of St Michael's, "I know it is useless, she will die as her sister has just done, and the first letter will bring me an account of her death." The Community made a most fervent novena; I did not join in it as I preferred to leave myself in the hands of God. God was pleased to hear their prayers; and in place of the news of my death, it was myself and a companion who presented ourselves at St. Michael's. Rev. Mother Jouve left me there to gather strength while she went first to Natchitoches and [p. 2] Baton Rouge to make her regular visit; Mother Hyacinth, the sister of Rev. M. Cutts, was her travelling companion. We left St. Michael's at the end of May and went up the Mississippi to St. Louis where Rev. M. Jouve made the regular visit; and taking Mme O'Neil with us, we embarked on the Missouri to go to Leavenworth, Kansas. We were dressed in a secular costume that was not of the latest style, and on the boat we were objects of much curiosity. As I spoke English, I got the full benefit of the remarks made. One lady seeing us all in black had much compassion for us and asked Where we were going? If that old lady (Mere Jouve) was our Mother? If our husbands were all dead and how we were going to support ourselves? And many more questions of a like nature. To the last mentioned question, I answered that our husbands were dead, and that we intended to open a school.

Reaching Leavenworth we went to the Palace of the Rt. Rev. Bp. Meige, S.J. [*sic*] and were most kindly received. The Palace was a frame house containing five or six rooms, the Church was also a frame structure. [p. 3] During the four or five days we remained there the Bishop sent for his choir in order to have singing at the Mass in our honor. Mme O'Neil made her Profession in the Church. I arranged the altar and when I tried to put canonical candle sticks on the candles struck the ceiling and fell down. The kindness and goodness shown us by the Bishop I can never forget. When we were leaving he provided a nice lunch and plenty of it which was fortunate.

Once more we started for St. Mary's, this time in a carriage. We were two days going there; and as the driver did not know the road, we went some distance out of the way and were obliged to retrace our steps. The first night we stopped at an inn. The Mistress of the house was a French woman and was very kind to us; the place was filled with the drivers of the ox-carts that carried provisions up the country to the forts. We could not even have one room to ourselves, but the woman gave us hers, and she slept with her baby on the floor in one corner. [p. 4] The room opened on a porch; it was near the close of the month of June, and the heat was so great that we were obliged to leave the door open during the night. On the porch the drivers of the ox-teams slept or rested, and the night air was filled with the sounds of cursing, swearing, talking, laughing and snoring. We went to lie down on the bed but found it was occupied by a host of unpleasant insects who caused Mother Jouve to retreat to a rocking chair where she passed the night in prayer. After riding on the prairies in the hot sun all day, that was but little rest. All were astir very early next morning, and we were obliged to take breakfast with all those rough men. I could not eat anything, and the one who sat next me was much concerned at it and in a rough but kindly way urged me to eat. The French woman had taken a fancy to me, insisting that she had known me in Paris. To prove it she said my name was Elizabeth. That was true, then she spoke of persons and [p. 5] places I knew nothing about for I had never been in France. After a little conversation with her, Mother Jouve found out that she had not been to the Sacraments for many years. After much persuasion and even tears, she at length gave a promise to go to Confession to the next priest who passed that way. She was faithful to this promise, as the priest stopped at St. Mary's and declared it was a wonderful conversion, for as he said "She was a great fish." Thus our painful journey caused that joy in heaven that our Lord promised for the conversion of a sinner. When we resumed our journey, the woman gave me two biscuits because I had not been able to eat [p. 6] my breakfast; and these with the remnants of the lunch that the kind Bishop had given us proved to be all the food we had for the day. At noon we stopped at the house of an Indian, but we could not make ourselves understood nor get anything to eat. The large bottle of milk which had been [p. 6] put in our suitcase the first day because of the heat had become spoiled; when the driver of the carriage found this out, he stopped, jumped down, caught one of the cows that were feeding on the prairie and filled our bottle with nice fresh milk, so we had something to drink with our lunch. About evening we reached the Mission where dear Mother Lucile and her little community of seven religious received us with open arms.

The Rev. Fathers also came to welcome us, the first white people we had seen that day. Seeing the poor little Mission consisting of two log houses resting on the ground, and containing only eight rooms, my heart failed me as I thought of the beautiful Convent of Grande [sic] Coteau, my first religious home where I had been so happy.

Completely exhausted by our journey we went very soon to rest, Rev. M. Jouve sharing her room with me. No sooner had we extinguished our candle than the crickets, who lived in the wide cracks of the floor, became very friendly [p. 7] even so far as to get on the beds and chirped with all their might so that sleep or rest was impossible. I got up and lit the candle remaining beside it to watch is as long as it burned so that Rev. Mere Jouve might get a little sleep.

The next morning was a Saturday. We went to the Church, which was built of logs, the walls covered with a coarse canvas, which was whitewashed; there was not enough to cover the entire ceiling so four pieces of brown canvas some distance apart were nailed up to complete it. A little girl seeing it asked her companion why they did that? She answered: Why don't you know that the Catholic Church has four marks by which you may know it; they show us that this is the true Church.

Rev. M. Jouve shed tears when she saw the poverty and dirt amidst which Our Lord dwelt for the love of us. She named me Sacristan, which gave me enough to do for everything was wanting. The next day, Sunday, [p. 8] we spent shaking hands with the Indians who welcomed us saying "Bon Jour." On Monday, I began to lead regular life; it was a busy one as I was Sacristan, Childrens' Vestier [sic], Class Mistress, had the three meals and recreations besides. When the little Indians came to us, they had no clothes, perhaps one little covering for modesty sake. Mother Lucile would take them to a little house set apart for that purpose, herself wash and comb them and put on them clothes from the vestry. To keep this supplied fell to my share, and I was aided by the larger girls who served beautifully. Every day the children heard Mass at a quarter-past six; after breakfast about a dozen of the large girls went to milk; six or seven accompanied them to carry home the milk, and about the same number churned; the others went to help in the kitchen or do the house work. All had some manual labor. At nine o'clock class began. We were only three teachers, so each had two divisions. At five o'clock the [p. 9] large girls again went to milk and to do the house work. The little girls remained with Mother Lucile and learned how to knit.

My class consisted of from twenty to twenty-five large girls. Some were very smart, others lazy and troublesome. They liked sewing, fancy work and music. One day an old Indian came to the convent and was so pleased at hearing someone play on the piano that he gave ten dollars and ordered his little daughter to take lessons. He was greatly disappointed that she did not learn to play in a few days. He was a very holy old man and always saw his Angel Guardian at his side and died singing the Magnificat.

Some of the Indians have great faith and are very pious. One summer we had no rain for a long time; the children were told to pray or they would have nothing to eat. One little girl on hearing this asked permission to go to the Church to pray for rain and, if the rain came, that she might receive a medal of the Blessed Virgin. [p. 10] The permission and promise were given and away she ran; shortly after her return from the Church the clouds gathered and the rain fell in great abundance. When she received the medal, she kissed it again and again with great joy.

Even the smallest children possess great endurance. A little girl of mine fell out of bed one night and broke her arm; she went back to bed, got up with the others, dressed herself as well as she could, went to Mass. It was only at breakfast time when I saw her eating with her left hand that I found out what was the matter. I took her to Mother Lucile who sent for the Dr. to set it.

One day they were playing in the grass when one of the little girls got a "picker" as they called it under her finger nail; it went in so far that we could not get it out, when the Dr. came he pulled the whole nail off; she [p. 11] did not cry, simply asked if it would get well soon.

At first I had a hard time, but soon I learned to manage them and I loved them. Those who lived near the Church went to Mass every day and to Confession on Saturday. Those that lived at a distance would come to Confession on Saturday and stay overnight with their friends. On feast days the Convent was full, they would sleep on the floor wrapped in their blanket and gave no trouble. At eight o'clock they had Mass during which they sang Canticles in the Indian language. We were obliged to go to the Church for all our Exercises. One day when I was making my adoration a big Indian with a knife at his side and a package in his arms came in; he looked around then stretched himself on a bench and opened his package, which proved to be of candy and deliberately ate it. I made a poor [p. 12] adoration that day. Another day I was alone there when a young white man came in and went up to the altar, examined the tabernacle, candlesticks etc. I thought he was looking for the key. I ran home and sent for one of the fathers from the College, but when I got back to the

Church he was gone and I found forty dollars under the tabernacle. We heard afterwards that he had studied for the priesthood but had lost his mind.

At Christmas and on New Year the whole tribe would come to shake hands, wish us a happy feast and receive a piece of candy and cake. They were very fond of sweet things. A boy once received five dollars for a present and spent the entire sum in candy, sat under the tree and ate it all himself.

As our houses were built of logs, there were air holes enough for wind, rain and rats. One night when it had been raining, I heard a queer noise and I got up when I found [p. 13] myself standing in water which reached above my ankles. One day the door of my sleeping room was left open, and a large snake entered and coiled itself around the leg of my bed. Fortunately, someone saw it and killed it before bed time. Such things often happened.

One night as Sister B. was going to bed, she heard a queer noise behind her bed; she lit a candle and found that a swarm of bees had entered through a crack and settled down. No one in the vicinity kept bees so we did not know where they came from. We put them in a box and in the course of time, we had a dozen swarms.

In the winter the cold was very severe: our beds were often covered with snow, and in the mornings we would sometimes find our bed clothes frozen around our mouths; frequently while at our meals the water would freeze in our glasses. We had [p. 14] many hard and disagreeable things to bear, but the certainty of doing the Holy Will of God made everything sweet and easy. I never prayed with more devotion than in that old Church even when trembling with cold.

The first year I was there at Christmas time I made a little "Crib" in the Church. The poor Indians had never seen such a thing and prayed near it with delight. One little by [sic] went crying to his mother and asked her to give him some money. She gave him a quarter and he ran to the "Crib" and said: "Here Blessed Virgin buy some clothes with this, for the Baby looks so cold." I left the money there for the others to see it and on the Feast of the Epiphany I had between ($) fifteen and twenty dollars, which I spent for the altar. Those were happy days spent purely for God, self was forgotten.

Senators, Agents and other visitors frequently came from Washington to examine the school. [p. 15]. On one occasion the Vice President and eight Senators on their way up the country stopped. They examined everything and were particularly pleased with the needlework. All wanted some article; the Vice President asked for a pair of moccasins. I took his measure and had them finished by the time he came back; he was much pleased with them. Many passenger trains to the Rocky Mountains also stopped, and the passengers destroyed everything within reach. Mother Lucile never refused anything asked of her. During her long and painful illness she never made a complaint and when death came accepted it with resignation. The Indians mourned over her like little children for their mother. She truly had a mother's heart for them. The old church was still used up to the time we left St. Mary's, and in it I made my Profession in 1862. I had no Probation as when there was question of it Father Deals S.J. [p. 16] said life at the Mission was Probation enough. We began to build a New Convent, and at that time there was question of the Indian tribes being sent to the Indian Territory.

The Mason who had charge of the building was a Free-Mason and watched us as carefully as he did the building; when it was completed he was evidently impressed for he told one of our Mothers that he was so well pleased with the kindness with which the Indian children were treated that if he had fifty children he would send them to us; later three of his children became Catholics.

When the new house was finished, it was very fine but we were so very poor and had no furniture. Mother Lucile had a straw chair, the only one in the house. The ladies of the town presented us with a dozen cane bottom chairs and tables for the parlors. When we opened the school in 1869, we had thirty-five boarders and eighty in the Parochial School. The Indian tribes were sent to the Reservation. [p. 17]

Shortly after going into the new house, Mother Lucile died; all the Indians came to the funeral each carrying a lighted candle. When the Jesuit College was burned down in 1879, they took our new house, and I was sent to Chicago and the rest of the community dispersed among the other houses of the Vicariate.

## 6. Memories of Ellen Craney, RSCJ (after 1879)

*English autograph, USCA*

S.C.J.M.
   St. Charles
   Aug. 7

*[In another hand:]*
Very valuable, a letter from Mother Ellen Craney, who lived at St. Mary's in her youth.

My dear Mother Thompson *(Mother Celeste T.)*
   What a delightful task you have set me, a work of love, truly! To me, Mother Lucille is a heroine, whose heroism is lost sight of in the shadow of her great exemplar, Ven M. Duchesne. In the early days of her life in the wilderness or on the borderland, when mortification was her daily, hourly companion, it was always borne and concealed with a smile, a smile that was an encouragement to those who labored with her. In her old age, when I knew her, she was suffering from a painful and humiliating disease which separated her a good deal from the community, to her intense grief, for her life was very lonely without us, but bowing to authority she went on her silent way to the end. She was of the wonderfully supernatural type to which all our first mothers belonged, and was truly befitting one whom our Saint-Mother sent in her name to the U.S.A.
   Now for a few words about the enclosed clippings and photos: the one of the tomb is rather dilapidated. This is because it was well pasted in a book, but I believe you can decipher the names by means of even a small magnifier. After they were taken

by Father McNien, S. J. a short time before his tragic death, they were very legible, but have grown dim under cover. They are,

| Sister Amiotte, (died 1857) | Madame Reegan[97] (died 1858) |
|---|---|
| Mother Mary Anne O'Connor (died 1864) ||
| Mother Lucille Mathevon (died 1876) ||
| Sister Mary Laton [sic] (died 1876) | Mother Deagan [sic] (died 1872) |
| Mother Boyle (died 1877) ||

Their remains are beneath the base. The little cross in ink indicates the place where the Jesuits are buried. If you can get a picture of present day St Marys, look well at the grand "Gym" – it is where our graveyard was. After we left there in 1879 the Jesuits removed the remains of our Religious to the City cemetery, erected the tombstone, and have ever since cared for it. The inscription is perfectly correct, for names and dates. The "Indians" I put in simply because the girl is a Pottawatomie. Her ancestors knew Mother Lucille, she did not.

In appearance Mother Lucille (it was only in her old age that I knew her) was not striking—what old person is? She was rather bent, but firm on her feet; complexion sallow; eyes large and bulging, the whites glazed; teeth remarkable, large, strong,

---

97 This is Catherine Regan, RSCJ, born in Ireland probably in 1831, died at St. Mary's, not in 1858, as Craney read the tombstone, but July 23, 1868, before final profession; the number is difficult to read. For further biographical information, see Chicoine, 113-114.

she never had a toothache! Kind and gentle she welcomed us with a sweet smile. She had been a great laugher in early days – a fact that helped much to carry her through pioneer difficulties and made her wonderfully forbearing. Think of it – I have her profession cross! It was indented and battered – all the dearer for that. As for the original houses, they were two story, or 1 ½, of planed logs, partitions of canvas or tenting, stairs fine walnut, from the forests. There were three houses. They looked like any ordinary frame houses. The largest was, I think, about 40 ft long and 20 wide (two rooms). Mother Lucille lived somewhere in this, and the Indians to honor their "Queen" often planted their totem poles with scalps on it before her door. The day she was buried the Indians, who had gathered from all the country round, hovered near her grave till nightfall, moaning, crying gently, the saddest looking people I ever saw. No wonder, what had she not done for them! She was the first white woman who put foot in what is now St. Marys. When the caravan came from Sugar Creek, 1848, the Fathers decided to plant the cross there, St. Marys; the lazy Indians were lolling around, not caring when the tents would be put up; then Mother Lucille jumped out of the wagon and began vigorously pulling up the long grass and weeds, to clear a place for our tent; that made the Indians ashamed, and a few sharp words from the Fathers, set them going, and our tent was soon up; theirs followed. The trouble always was that if they, i.e., priests and religious, wanted to hold the Indians, they always had to speak of them gently, kindly, soothingly, or they would decamp and go to the wild branch of the tribe.

In the early seventies our Mothers thought Mother Lucille should have a rest; they brought her to St. Charles. It nearly broke her heart, she sank rapidly, and to save her life it was decided that she would return to St. Marys. The news restored her, but when she reached her destination dismay followed; it was not her St. Marys! That fine new house had no charms for her. True, the old buildings were still there (in front of what is now the College) but everything about them was changed. With the old Sisters she lamented the fact that muddy shoes were not allowed in the hall, that furniture had to be handled gently etc. The Indians, too, had mostly moved farther away and she saw little of them. She realized what the near future would be, and it came, viz. the year we closed, not a child with a drop of Indian blood in her was in the school—the first time this happened. Mother Duchesne's efforts had come to an end. Mother Lucille's herculean work was over, our missionary career was finished, at least with the Indians.

My dear Mother, will this scribbling be of any use to you? There is no connection but you will put some in by using your logic and good style. Keep my little treasures as long as needed. I wish I could do more for you. I must put in a little remark I heard Father Conway, S.J. make. As a little boy he was the first and for long time the only white boy at St. Marys, with 90 Indians. He used to get tired of the rough company, and went over to the convent, sat down by M. L. put his head on her shoulder and cried. She patted and comforted him (his mother was dead) and he went back comforted. Only for M. L., he said, I could not have remained at St. M.

# PRIMARY SOURCES

### Notes on Primary Sources

Accounts of the beginnings of the mission at Sugar Creek are multiple and repetitive, yet each one distinct. Lucile herself seems to have written at least three accounts: two autographs [USCA], and a third, a letter to Madeleine Sophie Barat dated August 1841, a copy incorporated into the house journal. All are in French, translated here by C. Osiek.

The memoirs of Elizabeth Schrader, RSCJ (1829-1903), Ellen Craney, RSCJ (1853-1931) and Marie Monzert, RSCJ (1828-1903) are portraits from time spent with Lucile in her later years.

E. Schrader's and E. Craney's accounts in English autograph, USCA.

M. Monzert's account in French, typed copy and translation by unknown translator, both USCA, originally from GASSH.

The house journal [*HJ*] is a compilation of accounts and letters in French from the earliest years, the collection attributed to Catherine de Tardiu, RSCJ. From 1873, it is in English, written in a different hand. It includes short death notices of Mary Layton (1876), and Rosa Boyle (1877), and a longer one for Lucile, and substantial entries 1874 through the closing in 1879. The original copy is at USCA.

Translations, unless otherwise specified, are those of the authors.

**Primary sources**

Craney, Ellen, RSCJ (1853-1931), "Letter from Mother Ellen Craney, who lived at St. Mary's as a young religious, to Mother Celeste Thompson." August 7, undated; before 1926. Autograph. USCA IV.K Box 2. [Craney]

Duchesne, Rose Philippine, RSCJ, *Journal of the Society in America* 1818-1840. [*JSA*]

General Archives, Society of the Sacred Heart, Rome. [GASSH]

House Journal, Sacred Heart Convent, St. Mary's, Kansas. 1841-1879. Autograph USCA IV.K. Box 1 [*HJ*]

*Lettres Annuelles de la Société du Sacré-Cœur* 1841-1879 [*AL*]
    1869-1871. 2. 279-280 (return to St. Mary's)
    1876-1877. 2. 271-279 (death notice)

Mathevon, Lucile, « Commencement de la Mission Indienne » French Autograph. USCA IV.K Box 1

Mathevon, Lucile, « Journal de la fondation de la Maison du SC à Sugar Creek Indian Territory » French Autograph. USCA IV.K Box 1.

Monzert, Marie Rose, RSCJ (1828-1903). *Notes sur la vie de Mère Lucile Mathevon.* Typed copy French and English translation. USCA. XII.C Martinez Box 7. Original GASSH. [Monzert]

Deeds and acts of incorporation, Academy of the Sacred Heart, St. Marys, Kansas, 1869. Original copies. USCA IV.K Box 1.

Schrader (Shrader, Schroeder), Marie Elizabeth, RSCJ (1829-1903). Account of St. Mary's, Kansas. English Autograph. USCA. IV.K Box 2

United States-Canada Provincial Archives, St. Louis, Missouri. [USCA]

## Secondary Sources

Blish, Mary, RSCJ, and Carolyn Osiek, RSCJ. *Anna Xavier Murphy, RSCJ (1793-1836) Missionary to Louisiana.* Society of the Sacred Heart, 2021.

Cahier, Adele, RSCJ. *Vie de la Vénérable Mère Barat, Fondatrice et première supérieure de la Société du Sacré-Cœur de Jésus.* 2 vols. Paris: E. de Soye et Fils, 1884. [Cahier]

Callan, Louise, RSCJ. *The Society of the Sacred Heart in North America.* London/New York/Toronto: Longmans Green, 1937. [Callan]

Chicoine, Maureen J., RSCJ. *Grave on the Prairie; Seven Religious of the Sacred Heart and Saint Mary's Mission to the Potawatomi.* Society of the Sacred Heart, USC Province, 2018. [Chicoine]

De Charry, Jeanne, editor. *Correspondence, Saint Madeleine Sophie Barat – Saint Philippine Duchesne.* 4 vols. Rome: Pontifical Gregorian University, 1979-1981. Translated by B. Hogg, J. Sweetman, A. O'Leary, M. Coke. Rome: Society of the Sacred Heart, 1988-2000. [De Charry]

*Duchesne, Rose Philippine, RSCJ, Pioneer on the American Frontier (1769-1852), Complete Works.* Edited by Marie-France Carreel, RSCJ, and Carolyn Osiek, RSCJ; translated by Frances Gimber, RSCJ. 2 vols. Society of the Sacred Heart, 2019.

Garraghan, Gilbert J., S.J., *The Jesuits of the Middle United States.* 3 vols. Chicago: Loyola University Press, 1983-1984. [Garraghan]

Garvey, Mary, RSCJ, *Mary Aloysia Hardey, Religious of the Sacred Heart 1809-1886.* London: Longmans Green, 1925.

Kilroy, Phil, *Madeleine Sophie Barat: A Life.* Cork University Press/Paulist Press, 2000. [Kilroy]

O'Dowd, Mary, "Lucile Mathevon, Years among the Potawatomi." Unpublished paper, USCA, n.d., after 1970.

Paisant, Chantal, editor, *Les Années pionnières, 1818-1823: Lettres et Journaux des premières missionnaires du Sacré-Cœur aux États-Unis.* Paris : Les Éditions du Cerf, 2001. [Paisant]

*Religieuses du Sacré-Coeur: Quelques contemporaines de la Fondatrice.* Paris: Gigord, 1924. Lucile Mathevon, Vol. 1 pp. 107-137.

Schmidt, Kelly L., "Enslaved Faith Communities in the Jesuits' Missouri Mission," *U.S. Catholic Historian* 27:2 (2019) 49-81.

Thompson, Celeste, RSCJ, "Mother Lucile Mathevon among the Potawatomi." M.A. thesis, Loyola University, Chicago, 1926.

# INDEX OF BIOGRAPHICAL NOTES

Amiot, Louise ..................................................... 41
Anduze, Aristide, C.M. ...................................... 14
Armstrong, Mary Ann ...................................... 78
Cavanagh (Kavanagh), Marie Xavier ..... 128
Craney, Ellen ..................................................... 58
De Tardiu, Catherine ........................................ 84
Deegan, Julia ..................................................... 88
Delacroix, Charles ............................................ 17
Dowdall, Mary Teresa ...................................... 81
Du Rousier, Anna ............................................. 63
Dutour, Hélène ................................................... 8
Galitzine, Elisabeth ........................................... 38
Gallwey, Margaret Ann .................................... 65
Gauthreaux, Mary Rose ................................... 82
Guillot, Eulalie .................................................. 32
Hamilton, Eulalie Regis ................................... 15
Hoey, Margaret ................................................. 80
Jouve, Amelie .................................................... 60
Jouve, Euphrosine ............................................ 12
Knapp, Mary ..................................................... 17
Lalanne, Catherine ....................................... 9-10
Landry, Carmelite ............................................ 13
Martial, Bertrand ............................................ 108

153

McKay, Susannah .................................30
Miège, Jean Baptist, bishop ..........................66
Milmoe, Mary Ellen ..................................... 78
Monzert, Mary Rose ...................................62
Moulin(s), Marie ............................................ 6
Murphy, Anna Xavier ..................................... 8
O'Connor, Mary Ann .................................74
O'Neil, Bridget ............................................69
Palmer, Mary ..............................................84
Pratte, Bernard ............................................14
Regan, Catherine ........................................ 146
Schrader, Elizabeth .....................................69
Thiéfry, Catherine ...................................... 128
Van Quickenborne, Felix, SJ ........................ 18
Verhaegen, Peter, SJ .....................................19

www.ingramcontent.com/pod-product-compliance
Lightning Source LLC
Chambersburg PA
CBHW041142110526
44590CB00027B/4099